# SE𝒳Y ENCOUNTERS

## 21 Days of Provocative Passion Fixes

By Carole Pasahow, D.S.W., A.C.S.W.

Adams Media Corporation
Avon, Massachusetts

## Dedication

I DEDICATE THIS BOOK to my husband, Jim, who has been my best friend and passionate partner for the last thirteen years. Jim's consistent encouragement, feedback, and participation throughout this project were invaluable to its successful completion.

## Disclaimer

The patients described in the book are composites of real couples with specific sexual dysfunctions that have been successfully treated with the 21-Day Passion Fix Program. Although all the examples in this book include issues from real lives, none of them represent actual couples in my practice. Confidentiality was carefully respected in order to protect patients' privacy.

Published by Adams Media Corporation
57 Littlefield Street, Avon, MA 02322. U.S.A.
www.adamsmedia.com

ISBN: 1-58062-639-4

Printed in Canada.

J I H G F E D C B A

**Library of Congress Cataloging-in-Publication Data**
Pasahow, Carole.
Sexy encounters / by Carole Pasahow.
p.    cm.
ISBN 1-58062-639-4
1. Sex. 2. Interpersonal relations. 3. Intimacy (Psychology)  I. Title.
HQ21 .P248      2003
306.7--dc21      2002011336

This publication is designed to provide accurate and authoritative information with regard to the subject matter covered. It is sold with the understanding that the publisher is not engaged in rendering legal, accounting, or other professional advice. If legal advice or other expert assistance is required, the services of a competent professional person should be sought.
— From a Declaration of Principles jointly adopted by a Committee of the American Bar Association and a Committee of Publishers and Associations

Cover photograph ©David Stoecklein/Corbis

*This book is available at quantity discounts for bulk purchases.*
*For information, call 1-800-872-5627.*

# Contents

# CONTENTS

# *Foreword*

IN THIS ERA OF "FASTER IS BETTER," there is one thing that I consistently hear from clients, read on my massive message boards at iVillage.com, and discuss during my numerous guest appearances on national television and radio shows (including my own weekly Web radio show at iVillage). People are complaining that there is "no time for sex."

The 1999 *Journal of the American Medical Association* study showed that four out of ten women and three of ten men suffer from sexual dysfunctions, most of which can be treated if a person or couple can find the appropriate resources and make the time to fix what ails them. For more than twenty-five years, I have treated the three most common sex problems: No orgasm (for women), erectile dysfunction or early ejaculation (for men), and low desire (for both).

Most of it boils down to three common themes:
1. I have no time for sex.
2. I've/we've lost the spark in our relationship.
3. I'm not sure how to get our sex life back on track.

Many couples feel that having sex involves a level of sexual gymnastics and a demand for attention to their partner's sexual needs, which they find depleting, overwhelming, and a good reason to avoid sex completely.

Sex therapy techniques today encompass a plethora of new pills or medically based sexual aids, and behavioral or talk-only approaches. These include sensate focus, temporary abstinence from sexual intercourse, regrouping life priorities, and a bulging marketplace filled with fancy new consumer-friendly sex toys to try in the bedroom.

Pop magazines, radio, and TV talk shows are bursting with stories that encourage sexual experimentation, name new body positions, push exciting new techniques, and tout new discoveries for life between the sheets. Even the age-old "weekly sex date" (often recommended by sexuality experts for couples with a lagging sex life) can easily go stale under the pressure to meet unreasonable demands and media-exploited expectations for sexual athletics.

Then comes along a book that really does the job: *Sexy Encounters*. Dr. Pasahow's book works, because it's based on four basic ingredients:

1. **Common sense:** keeping it simple and doable for real people; recognizing that most people are just too busy to do much more than they already do.
2. **Quick-fix approach:** using time-limited encounters and tightly prescribed activities; creating time-saving devices for better sex.
3. **Positive emphasis** on play, on foreplay (anticipating, building desire, fantasy) and on whole-body sex, versus genital mechanics.

4. **Encouraging communication and negotiation skills**, which inherently build intimacy, including weekly before-and-after sharing.

What I love about Pasahow's approach is how it takes the pressure off for couples to have sexual intercourse as the goal of sex, away from the often misplaced emphasis on genital geometry. By skipping the demands for penis-in-vagina sex, couples become more receptive to exploring whole-body sex, often where reconnection really occurs.

Dr. Pasahow's idea of a ten-minute limit to the prescribed encounters opens the gate for more, while removing the enormous barriers for most couples to go the distance.

I love the simplicity that Carole Pasahow uses to guide her points. Her patients' stories amuse us, while enlightening us, and her readers will feel greater comfort, joy, and ease in lighting the spark that will create the flames of sexual erotic pleasure.

I have known the author for more than twenty years, as a colleague and a friend. I've admired her keen mind, felt her kind heart, delighted in her warm humor, and watched her powerful presence shine—helping her patients and her colleagues with whom she shares her wisdom. I know that *Sexy Encounters* will bring fresh hope to your life. It's a fun, practical model for rekindling (or finding for the very first time) the pleasures of the flesh and hot romance.

—Dr. Patti Britton
Los Angeles, CA, Summer 2002

# Acknowledgments

I AM SO GRATEFUL to all the people who were supportive and offered consistent encouragement during this project. I want to again thank my husband, Jim, and children Nicole, Kenny, Eva, and Andrew for being so understanding of my time commitment to this book. I am always grateful to my parents, Lola and Jerry Pasahow, who have always been supportive of my career, and most recently, the Passion Fix. They are the ones who taught me by example how important it is to make time for your partner and keep the passion flowing.

Thank you to the many soccer families on the Torpedoes Soccer team in Wyckoff, New Jersey, as well as my close friends, not only for their enthusiasm for the project, but also for reinforcing my belief in the value of a program to keep a sexual relationship vibrant even when there's no time for sex! An important acknowledgement to my dear friend, Diane Sobin, who was the one who first came across the cartoon of the DINS couple (Double Income, No Sex) in the January 1, 2000 *Wall Street Journal*. This acronym has since become an integral part of the project. Thank you, Diane.

Central to making this book a reality are my wonderful

patients who shared the most personal and intimate aspects of their lives as couples and participated in the treatments that formed the basis of the Passion Fix. They were enthusiastic about the book from the start and felt that it was important to share their own journey of achieving great sex through the program.

Many thanks to the late Helen Singer Kaplan, M.D., Ph.D., and her talented teaching staff at the Human Sexuality Program, New York Hospital–Cornell Medical Center: Merle Kroop, M.D.; Sharon Nathan, Ph.D.; Elaine Kleinbart, M.S.W.; Michael Perelman, Ph.D.; and others, who through their brilliant tutelage helped me develop the skills to heal the most intimate and devastating problem a couple can face, their sexual relationship.

Thank you, Irwin Epstein, Ph.D., and the faculty of Hunter College, School of Social Work, for assisting me with my clinical dissertation, which allowed me to better understand how couples best develop intimacy. Much appreciation to Mark T. Schaefer, Ph.D., and David H. Olson, Ph.D., for the use of their Pair Inventory and Edward M. Waring, M.D., for the use of The Waring Intimacy Questionnaire. Modified forms of these inventories were used as assessment measures, interventive strategies, and outcome measures in my clinical dissertation. These became the basis for the sex life checkup in the Passion Fix.

A special thank you to my dear friend and talented colleague, Patti Britton, Ph.D., for her continued support and resourcefulness in the field of Sexual Enhancement. I am flattered to have her write the foreword to my book.

Thank you to my good friend and associate Burton C. Schucker, Ph.D., for his never-ending support and time in giving me valuable feedback on the Passion Fix. Also thank you Beverly Whipple, Ph.D., R.N., F.A.A.N., for your enthusiasm and encouragement during this project. Thank you Steve Conley, Ph.D., and the entire AASECT staff and members for their support. Also thank you for giving me the opportunity to present a portion of my book at the AASECT annual conference.

Another thank you to Lilyan Wilder and Bob Berkowitz for their encouragement and guidance during this project.

A special thanks to my agent Nancy Love who believed in the project from the beginning and was most generous with her time and encouragement. Another very special thanks to the talented Susan Crain Bakos whom I met in my journey of trying to make my program a reality. Susan, being an expert writer in sexual journalism, found my program refreshing and unique and encouraged me to bring the program alive in book form. She generously taught me about the publishing world, and was kind enough to describe the Passion Fix in many of her magazine articles, with a feature article all about the program in March, 2001 *Redbook* "The Sex Trick Busy Couples Swear By." I am so flattered by her unfailing interest in the project and always grateful for her guidance. Thank you, Kristen Kemp, for your continued interest and belief in my work and for including Passion Fix suggestions in your article "My No. 1 Piece of Sex Advice Is . . . " for *Glamour* magazine (October, 2001).

Thank you, Claire Gerus, my editor, for her expertise, her patient and pleasant manner, and especially her careful guidance. I also want to acknowledge Laura MacLaughlin, Copy Chief, and Khrysti Nazzaro, Assistant Production Editor, for their responsiveness in working with me on the editing of this book and for the terrific final product. I'm so grateful to Adams Media for their continued interest in my ideas and putting so much of their time and interest into this book.

# *What Is the Passion Fix?*

MORE OFTEN THAN NOT the couple sitting across from me in my office is there because they aren't having as much good sex as one or both of them would like. They don't feel erotically connected. Maybe they have intercourse once a week, but they complain "the passion" is missing. Maybe they haven't made love in a month, several months, a year, or longer, in which case fear of failure keeps them apart as effectively as if they were wearing his and hers chastity belts and the keys were lost somewhere in the attic or the basement or perhaps the garage.

Sometimes the event propelling them into therapy is a seemingly insignificant one. A thirty-five-year-old wife wistfully described her pang of envy when she noticed another couple, the same age and married for the same number of years as she and her husband, exchange a highly charged look across a crowded room.

"She ran her tongue over her bottom lip, then blew him a kiss. I just knew they were going to make passionate love to each other that night," she said. She blinked back tears. "And I want what they have, what we used to have."

The wistful wife was referring to the intense erotic connection that every couple, if they are being honest with themselves and each other, wants to have. They want passion. And, they don't have it. When they come for help, they're really asking: *Can you fix the passion?*

One-half of that twosome sitting uncomfortably apart in my office will often answer my question "Why aren't you having regular satisfying sex?" with "We don't have time; and we're too tired when we finally do get time." The other will nod sadly in agreement. It's not uncommon for one or both of the parties to report having entirely lost interest in sex. She or he may say, "I wouldn't care if I never had sex again, but I know my partner would be upset."

I hear a common litany of excuses: "no time," "no energy," "too busy," "too stressed." Fatigue and stress are the natural byproducts of our modern lives, in which a marriage contains two people, two jobs, and numerous conflicting family obligations to growing children, aging parents, friends, and community—and not nearly enough time for each other. How does anyone have sex these days? Very few couples have "the time" when it comes to sex.

And, sometimes "too tired," "too busy," "no energy," and "too stressed" are acceptable excuses that hide the real problem. Performance anxiety, difficulty reaching orgasm, poor technique, a history of performance failures, or an inability to communicate needs and desires suppress sexual expression in many relationships. For couples with these problems, therapy may be a last resort after one partner has said to the other, "If you won't go with me to get help, I'm leaving you."

Whether a couple has good sex but no time or hides a

disappointing sex life behind an excuse, I do have the Passion Fix for them. A good sex life helps any couple deal more effectively with all the things that are keeping them apart, from the pressures and responsibilities of an overscheduled life to deeply rooted personal psychological or relationship issues. Good sex brings them together and helps them become healthier, mentally and physically.

"Good sex," I tell them, "is the penicillin for your relationship."

Most couples believe this is true in general. They just don't know how to make it come true for them. I know I can help them because I've helped hundreds of couples, with partners ranging in age from eighteen to eighty-four, including some who hadn't been sexually active together for several years before coming into the office. In fact, I've developed a twenty-one-day sexual enhancement program that can improve any couples' sexual relationship in as little as one hour (total) per week.

Before I outline the details of the 21-Day Passion Fix program for them, I have to dispel some of the common myths about what makes a good sex life. The first myth: *A good sexual encounter begins with a romantic seduction, moves into lengthy foreplay prior to intercourse, and ends with extended afterplay.* If they believe that, they're only going to have sex a few times a year when they can get away for at least a long weekend. In working with couples who rarely have time for romantic getaways, I've learned that effective treatment has to be fast and fun, and the homework assignments must be brief, but hot, hot, hot.

And, most of all, the program has to fit into the "real time" in a couple's daily life, not the occasional long weekend or summer vacation. Conventional sex advice doesn't work for them because it ignores that basic criterion. Typically, couples who have no time for sex are told to spend more romantic time together, but what they really need to learn is how to fit great sex into the time they have.

"Make dates with each other," the experts say. "Leave explicit sexy messages on her voice mail at the office." "Stuff love notes in his lunch bag or briefcase." Although these recommendations are loving gestures, they aren't innovative solutions to any couple's sex problems.

Another myth: *Courtship behavior, like bringing home the single perfect rose, will lead to great sex.* This myth may be true if you and your partner haven't been together very long. In fact, sex leads to romance for established couples, not vice versa.

I built a program based on two concepts that do work: Fantasy and the Quickie. Couples learn to use the Fantasy Encounter as mental foreplay, which arouses them for the Provocative Encounters, or Quickies.

"But I don't fantasize," some women—and men, too—insist. "How can I make this program work for me?"

You have erotic fantasies and sexual thoughts throughout the day. Everyone does. You may not know that you have them, but you do. Perhaps you habitually repress them. Maybe you're afraid of your fantasies because sometimes they aren't pretty or don't star your partner in life. There's nothing wrong with such fantasies. But they aren't the kind of fantasies you'll learn to create and use in the program.

And, why the Quickie?

This Quickie, the Provocative Encounter, is not your grandmother's quickie. It's designed to arouse and satisfy her as well as him. And it's designed to fit into the time available, the real time in your life.

We live most of our lives within the work week, with time and energy constraints continually imposed upon us. That "not vacation time" is the arena for creating lasting sexual change. You can't put your sexual relationship on hold like a home repair project and pick it up again when there's time.

For millions of couples, the lack of a satisfying sex life festers beneath the surface of their cooperative partnerships, breeding quiet anger and hidden resentment. Soon each feels frustrated and neglected by the other. Maybe that's already happening in your relationship.

Give me one hour a week for three weeks—and I can change your sex life, and your life, for the very much better.

# PART ONE

# THE SE𝒳 LIFE CHECKUP

*Chapter 1*

# How Do You Rate Your Sex Life?

THIS QUESTION is often answered with a self-deprecating joke. *Rate it? I can't even remember it.* Or, *What sex life—I'm married.* Or, *On a scale of one to ten, I'd give it a minus ten.*

When they take the question seriously, most couples admit that their sex life is far from an erotic disaster zone. Lovemaking isn't without its pleasures. There just aren't enough of them anymore.

The partners probably still find each other desirable—or at least they can recall what they found desirable once upon a time. They likely know how to arouse and please each other. In most relationships, neither partner suffers from a serious dysfunction like prolonged impotence (in the man) or chronic inability to reach orgasm (in the woman). They may have experienced difficulties with his erections and her orgasms, but they don't describe the erection and the orgasm as "unattainable" sexual events. Often they blame stress and fatigue, overcrowded schedules, and the burdens of family and job responsibilities for preventing them from fully enjoying sex. They don't blame each other.

Most couples who aren't entirely happy with their sex lives want more sex, more passionate sex, and more interesting and varied sex. Something may be "missing," but that doesn't make the whole sexual relationship bad. They want to fix the sex, not forget about it.

Whether their complaints about sex are as basic and specific as "not enough oral sex" or "too routine," the average couple initially expresses their unhappiness with the situation in broad, sweeping terms: *We never have time for sex. We always do it the same way.* Some couples may blame each other, hurling accusations in anger or frustration. They replace the inclusive and loving *we* with the judgmental *you,* as in, *You never want to do it anymore. You never take the time to please me.*

*Always* and *never* are rarely accurate terms, whether the couple is mutually accepting responsibility for the lack of satisfying sex—or blaming each other.

## *Why Can't They Define the Sex Problem?*

Many couples can't figure out what's wrong, as individuals or as a couple. They aren't able to sit down together and have a calm, thoughtful, positive discussion about making sex better, because neither has a list to bring to the table. Some couples can identify their problems—individually—but they don't know how to have that conversation with each other. She knows what's bothering her. He knows what's bothering him. But neither one knows how to broach the subject.

Couples who appear to have little else in common with

hundreds of other couples all tend to avoid the Sex Talk—especially when they need to have one.

It's easier to grumble, "I'm unhappy with our sex life," than to say, "I want to make love twice a week, not once a month," or "I want more oral sex sometimes, instead of intercourse."

Even couples with good communication skills can have difficulty communicating when the subject is sex. Identifying the problem is hard enough. Asking for change is a bigger challenge. A man or woman may throw out subtle seductive hints, but the other partner, harried and frazzled, doesn't catch them. Or each may secretly fantasize and long for a certain kind of lovemaking, not realizing that the other has hidden desires and longings as well. *Why doesn't he know what I want?* she wonders. Well, he wonders the same thing about her.

## Why Do Intimate Partners Have So Much Trouble Talking about Sex?

Sexuality is intrinsic to identity. When we talk about sex, we're talking about our truest selves. We think we can isolate erotic activity into the area described as our "sex life," but we can't. Sexuality permeates every aspect of an intimate relationship in much the same way French perfume scents a boudoir. Discussing something as important to personal identity and the relationship as sex makes everyone involved intensely vulnerable. This is the place where we can all be hurt badly. And how do most of us respond to the fear of being hurt? By protecting ourselves, not by opening up.

To make matters worse, few couples are fluent in the language of sex when they do discuss it. Some are too embarrassed to talk openly about techniques, positions, practices, and frequency. They may have grown up in sexually repressive families or had negative early sex experiences. Other couples can make sexual jokes and innuendoes and use graphic words for genitals and sex practices, but they can't stop using humor as a defense mechanism and talk *honestly* about sex. In fact, most couples circle warily around the subject, avoiding by mutual, if silent, consent their own taboo topics, like her difficulty reaching orgasm or his tendency to ejaculate too quickly. They talk around each other's sensitive places until one partner gets angry or hurt and accuses the other of being a "cold" or "selfish" lover. A cruel or simply thoughtless remark turns what could have been a loving request into a hurtful criticism.

Many people don't talk freely about sex because they fear rejection if they ask for what they want in bed. Nothing is more devastating than intimate rejection! So they give vague clues, share part but not all of what they want to say, or couch their desires in impersonal terms.

*If I tell her I want her to talk dirty to me, she'll be disgusted*, he thinks. *If I ask him to perform cunnilingus more often, he'll think I'm greedy*, she fears. "I'm horny," he says, hoping she'll open her arms, nuzzle his neck, and give him the entrée he needs to suggest lovemaking. She doesn't respond to what feels like a cold, impersonal demand. She's hurt because he didn't say, "I want you. I need you. I love you."

How many thousands of erotic opportunities are missed in relationships every hour of every day because someone didn't say the "right" word or make the "right" physical gesture?

## Why Do You Have to Rate Your Sex Life?

The 21-Day Passion Fix program is based on a simple premise: You can revitalize your sex life in one hour per week for three weeks by having one Fantasy Encounter and three Provocative Encounters (the new "Quickies").

You will design the encounters, with a great deal of help and inspiration from this book. First, however, you have to identify the problems in your sex life and target the solutions to those problems as your sexual goals. Every encounter helps you reach your goal, whether that goal is more sex, better technique, increased desire, heightened arousal, or something else.

You need the answers to create your sexual goals and fix the passion problem in your relationship.

## Can You Fix It Even If You Can't Talk about It?

You can't.

Before you and your partner can begin the 21-Day Passion Fix program, you *must* talk openly, honestly, and comfortably about sex. That's why you can't skim over the following questionnaire without answering the questions. These questions are designed to open an erotic dialogue between the two of you. Once you can talk about your sex life, you can identify the strengths and weaknesses in your relationship. Each of you must answer the questions. This isn't a magazine quiz in which she can guess how he might answer the question *What is her secret sex wish?*

Comparing and discussing your answers will take the fear, the sting, and the anger out of that Sex Talk you've been avoiding. The questionnaire is the hardest part of the program, but it's rewarding, exhilarating work. The answers are the basis for designing your 21-Day Passion Fix. You'll almost certainly learn something new, even surprising, about each other. And you won't be bored.

What if your partner doesn't want to take the quiz?

## How to Get Your Partner Involved

You need his or her active participation to make this program work. Assume that any reluctance he or she exhibits is nothing more than fear. You are the fearless partner; and you can afford to play the gentle leader. Your success depends on a good, nonthreatening presentation. Here's how:

1. *Employ shameless gender targeting in your sales pitch.* Women are typically the leaders in communication issues. If he is the reluctant partner, grab his interest by the metaphorical testicles. Men like to hear about good sex. You will gain his cooperation by saying, "Honey, I want more [better] sex. Don't you want that too? *(He will nod enthusiastically.)* The Passion Fix program sounds like fun. We have to promise to have three Quickies a week. *(More enthusiastic nodding.)* But the questionnaire is the first step. Won't you do it with me?"

If she is the one unwilling to take the quiz, substitute *Provocative Encounters* for *Quickies*.

2. *Respect your partner's sensibilities.* Some men and women are more sensitive than others. For example, a man or woman who is insecure as a lover may view any suggestion for improving the sexual relationship as a direct criticism of his or her lovemaking abilities. An inhibited partner may feel threatened by the prospect of erotic change. Protect your partner's self-esteem.

Say, "I love so much about our sexual relationship, like the way you kiss and caress me." Then describe the Passion Fix program as a way of enhancing the good sex you already enjoy.

3. *Actively solicit answers.* If your partner won't answer the questions in writing, take notebook and pen in hand and play reporter. Ask the questions. Turn the questionnaire into an amusing activity. Flatter when you can.

Say, "I know how you'd answer the question, 'Does your partner find you attractive and sexy?' That would have to be yes."

4. *Don't pressure.* You want to stimulate your partner's interest in joining you on an erotic journey. You won't accomplish that by psychological or emotional force or coercion. Try the subtle approach. Leave the book and a notebook containing your answers to the quiz questions lying on the bedside table.

Say, "Would you like to hear my ideas about how we could make our sex life hotter? I got these ideas from answering questions about sex and guessing how you might answer the same questions." Surely that will elicit a conversation.

5. Try *bribery*. Say, "Honey, we'll have sex more often if you answer these questions. I said *IF.*"

## *The Questionnaire*

I've grouped the questions into sections. In each section, you'll find examples, taken from my practice, of men and women who answered these questions in a certain way. To help you in your analysis, I give some general evaluations that can be reached from similar responses.

There are no right or wrong answers. Your honest responses will be the basis for creating your personalized 21-Day Passion Fix plan. By comparing what he says and what she says, a couple will see where they agree and disagree on sexual issues, what they want to change, and what they want to keep the same, only better. View the gap between those viewpoints *not* as the conflict zone, but as a land of erotic opportunity that you can cross together.

And a final note: Many sex questionnaires ask participants to answer the questions by checking *always, sometimes, frequently, rarely,* or *never.* The assumption is that multiple choice allows for less rigid responses than *yes* or *no.* I want you to answer these questions as you would the essay questions on school exams. Expound. The more you can share with your partner, the better.

## *Sexual Attraction and Desire*

Attraction brought you together. It's the necessary foundation of a good sex life. *Desire* is typically defined in the literature on sexuality as the spontaneous interest in having sex,
that diffused feeling of longing. (Arousal can occur without
desire, but we'll get into that later.) Lack of desire has been the
number-one presenting problem in sex therapy for many
years. Some desire problems are physical, including fatigue,
the side effects of medication, abuse of alcohol or drugs, and
hormonal imbalances associated with menstruation, post-
partum, menopause—even the use of birth control pills.
Often there are underlying personal and relationship issues.
Some couples are affectionate, yet they no longer find each
other sexually attractive or experience desire.

1. Does your partner seem interested in making love
   to you?
2. Do you feel appreciated by your partner?
3. Is your partner thoughtful and considerate of you?
4. Are you thoughtful and considerate of your partner?
5. Does your partner compliment you often?
6. Do you have romance in your relationship?
7. Do you find your partner attractive and sexy?
8. In your opinion, does your partner find you attractive
   and sexy?
9. Are you affectionate with each other?

If you and your partner don't find each other attractive and
sexy, you have little or no motivation to behave in romantic
ways. It's unlikely that you experience sexual desire for each

other, though either or both of you may feel desire for sex in general. So, you have sex, at least occasionally. But the sex feels perfunctory and impersonal.

When attraction fades, many couples become less thoughtful and considerate. The compliments drop off as well. Some couples stop treating each other like lovers because they have difficulty integrating new roles after children are born. Or they don't know how to balance their professional and personal lives when their careers become more demanding. Or they simply fall into the habit of taking each other for granted. Responsibilities seem more important than sex and romance.

### The Examples
*The "We Don't Have Time/Energy" Couple*
Diane and Charlie, two professionals in their thirties, said they had no time to dress to please each other at home or share a romantic dinner together or demonstrate affection, much less have sex, because they were too busy juggling their careers and their responsibilities as parents of two young children. "When we're not working," Diane said, "we're running in opposite directions carpooling the kids to soccer, dance class, and other activities too numerous to mention." Charlie added, "After we've done everything, we're too tired and irritable for the niceties, like whispering sweet nothings to each other."

When I asked them to compliment one another, Charlie said, "My wife is a good mother and a successful woman," and Diane said, "My husband is a good provider and a good father."

They defined themselves as parents and financial providers. Like many couples, they put achieving success while being devoted parents ahead of sharing a romantic and erotic personal relationship. They probably didn't receive positive messages about sexuality from their parents who likely believed that sex and romance were extraneous to a lasting marriage. No wonder they failed to recognize that many of their personal conflicts either resulted from, or were exacerbated by, underlying feelings of sexual frustration. Neither felt desired by the other.

Diane's frustration did become obvious when she said angrily to Charlie: "I could hire any devoted professional mother type to fill my shoes. Give you someone who carries her financial weight and takes care of the kids—and you'll be happy."

### The Mismatched Desire Couple

Paul secretly considered himself an inadequate lover to his wife, Sarah, the more overtly sexual partner. Although he perceived her as sexy and attractive in spite of the fact that she was thirty pounds heavier than she had been when he'd married her ten years earlier, he didn't rate himself as equally desirable. "She's sexually demanding," he complained, not recognizing that his failure to respond to her desire was rooted in his own feelings of inadequacy. As a mate, he was asexual, even childlike. Sarah grew frustrated and angry with him. When she tried to suppress her feelings, she ate. She used food to squelch her anger and dull her sense of sexual frustration. Eventually her desire decreased. Sadly, the more sexual partner in this kind of relationship commonly loses erotic motivation.

When a woman (or a man) gains weight, disregards personal appearance, and feels "unattractive," she may suffer from low self-esteem or have another problem separate from any relationship issue. She might, for example, have difficulty reconciling her role as mother with that of her husband's lover. Or she might be gaining that weight as a defense against a sexually rejecting partner or one who doesn't satisfy her when they do make love. It's not unusual for one or both partners to gain weight or behave in ways the other person finds sexually unappealing to avoid the issue of sex. And that gives the other partner yet another excuse for saying, "No."

"I might make love to her more often if she weren't fat," Paul said. "What difference does it make if I'm fat?" Sarah countered. They had turned her weight into the problem, not the symptom.

### The Almost Have-It-All Couple

Andrea and Steve, both forty, are one of those enviable couples who still find each other sexually attractive. They are affectionate, thoughtful, and complimentary of each other. Although they both work at demanding jobs and have two teenage sons, they still find time for candlelit dinners and the occasional weekend getaway.

"Our relationship is good in general," Andrea said. "So is our sex life," Steve added. But she said, "We don't make love as often as we did. Maybe we're in a bit of a rut." "Yes," Steve finished for her. "We are in a rut. Our sex life could use an energizing jolt. But we never thought about seeing a sex therapist because we don't have any real problems."

Like the other two couples, Andrea and Steve are ideal candidates for the 21-Day Passion Fix program. They have good enough sex, but they want more and better sex.

13

## *Arousal and Performance*

Sometimes desire is present, but it doesn't lead to arousal. Or, a man or woman may lose arousal after lovemaking begins. Causes for arousal problems can include the following:

- Inexperience, in young couples or new lovers
- Poor technique or a lovemaking style that doesn't suit the partner
- Fear of trying something new, which leads to boredom with the sexual routine
- Embarrassment about asking for what is needed to heighten or sustain arousal
- Physical problems, such as fatigue or the side effects of medication or psychological or emotional problems, like unexpressed anger and resentment toward the partner
- Performance anxiety, often rooted in a history of erection problems (For both men and women, the pressure to please the partner can produce performance anxiety.)

1. Do you become aroused easily, or do you have difficulties with arousal?
2. Does your partner become aroused easily or have difficulties with arousal?
3. Does he have more than an occasional problem getting or sustaining an erection?
4. Does she respond to his erectile difficulties in a way that makes him feel bad?
5. Do you and your partner know how to excite each other?
6. Do either of you feel anxious about "performing" adequately as a lover?

## The Examples

### The Prince and Princess Syndrome

Sophie sounded like many other women when she said, "If I have to ask Jeff for what I want in bed, I feel like a sex teacher. Giving him directions takes all the romance out of lovemaking. He should just know what to do."

"She refuses to be an active participant in sex," Jeff shot back. "But she doesn't mind criticizing me when it's over. How romantic is that?"

Sophie couldn't ask for what she wanted, but she focused obsessively on her hidden desires whenever Jeff began making love to her. Whatever he did wasn't "right" because it didn't match her imagined erotic scenario. Consequently, she had difficulty becoming aroused. She was the fairy tale princess waiting for Prince Charming's perfect kiss. But no one had given the hapless prince his training manual.

### The Insecure Lover

Rosie came to see me because her partner, Jim, repeatedly told her that she wasn't getting excited enough during sexual encounters. "What can I do to please you?" he begged. He didn't believe her when she insisted she was pleased.

"I'm not a moaner," Rosie admitted, "but I do enjoy our lovemaking. I lubricate. I reach orgasm. I'm satisfied. Why doesn't he read those signs instead of listening for the noises I don't make? He pays too much attention to my reactions."

Jim needed proof of his partner's passion because he felt inadequate as a lover. Once Rosie understood that, she stopped feeling as if she were under a microscope and began communicating her sexual pleasure through louder moans, signs, and exclamations. Their situation could easily have had another outcome, like sexual withdrawal on both sides. Performance anxiety is insidious. Eventually Jim would likely have experienced difficulty in achieving and maintaining an erection, while Rosie's arousal would have become inhibited by his overwhelming attention to his flagging penis.

### The Affectionate Couple

Stan and Marsha, a couple in their mid-thirties who'd been together since high school, had a "comfortable sex life." On their first visit, Marsha said, "We don't regard a sexual encounter as a performance, but rather as an opportunity to express our affection." Stan said, "We have a satisfying sexual and emotional intimacy with each other; and we enjoy making love."

No anxiety. No performance problems. No loss of desire or lack of attraction. Why were they there? Not enough excitement! "We'd like to jazz things up in the bedroom once in a while," Stan said. "Maybe we've become a little too predictable," Marsha acknowledged.

Enhanced erotic communication, one aspect of the 21-Day Passion Fix program, dramatically improved the sex lives of all three of these couples.

## Communication and (Emotional and Sexual) Intimacy

Couples need good communication skills to be truly intimate, on an emotional as well as sexual level. Intimacy is the continuously evolving outcome of disclosure and acceptance. In a strong intimate relationship, each partner can risk self-disclosure without fear of being judged or putting the relationship at risk.

When partners don't communicate, they often begin building emotional walls around themselves. Couples begin to guess at each other's true meanings and motives. Distrust develops. They don't feel close to each other. So how can the sex be great?

1. Can you express your sexual needs without feeling awkward?
2. Can you listen to your partner's sexual needs without making judgments?
3. Do you feel emotionally closer to your partner after lovemaking?
4. Does your partner listen when you need to talk?
5. Are you willing to listen when your partner needs to talk?
6. Can you tell your partner anything without being judged?
7. Can you state your feelings without getting defensive?
8. Do you often feel distant from your partner?
9. Does your partner understand your hurts and joys?
10. Do you feel angry with your partner most of the time?
11. Do you feel that you and your partner's conflict resolution skills are good or poor?

## The Examples
### The "Walking on Eggshells" Syndrome
Lori and Stuart, attractive professionals in their late thirties, behaved more like critical parents than loving spouses.

"I feel like I've been walking on eggshells our whole marriage," Stuart said. "No matter what I do for her, it isn't good enough—especially in bed." Lori retorted that he was "unduly critical." "He makes me feel stupid," she said. The emotional and sexual distance between them was a yawning chasm.

Their situation is not unusual. A lot of couples feel as if the floors of their marriages are carpeted in eggshells. The adult children of critical parents, Lori and Stuart had let the repeating of old patterns control their lives. Each felt misunderstood by the other. Each retreated to the safety of distance positions, which they maintained by frequent arguing and withholding emotional information.

### The "She Talks, but He Won't Hear" Couple

Terri, thirty-four, gave her husband, Peter, forty-eight, an ultimatum: therapy or divorce. "He doesn't want to hear anything I have to say about sex," Terri said. "He shuts me down in every way." Her needs and desires, Peter countered, weren't "normal."

She'd tried asking for what she wanted both in and out of bed—to no avail. "I want to make love wearing nothing but a black lace garter," Terri said. "I want him to come to bed in black jockey shorts." Suggestions like that make him angry because "dressing up for sex isn't normal." Peter was even less responsive when Terri asked him to touch or kiss her in a certain place or way during lovemaking. "That spoils the mood for me," he explained. "I lose my sexual focus."

Peter, who is fourteen years older than Terri, was threatened by her ease in communicating sexual needs. He believed he should be the aggressive partner, the experienced one with

18

creative sexual ideas, but his beautiful young wife was playing his role. Putting Terri down when she made sexual requests gave Peter the sexual distance he required for concealing his fear of inadequacy.

### The Withholding Pattern

Neil and Lois, in their late thirties, were married fifteen years when he told her he'd had enough of her "withholding" behavior. "She won't give me sex if she isn't feeling close to me," Neil said. "And she doesn't feel close to me unless I'm 'sharing' my feelings with her." Lois countered with a classic statement: "He never talks about his feelings." Each felt rejected by the other.

Later Lois admitted that, yes, he did sometimes talk about his feelings—typically after lovemaking. Many men don't feel emotionally close to their partners unless they experience sexual intimacy. Through sex, they feel accepted and loved, making them able to open up verbally during afterplay. Some women, on the other hand, have an opposing perspective. They need emotional closeness, defined in verbal terms, to enjoy sexual intimacy. Couples can find themselves in a sexual standoff if they don't learn how to give each other some ground.

Self-esteem issues prevented these couples from learning more about their partner's sexual needs. Because they didn't confront the issues directly, they began having sex less often. Ironically, more frequent and satisfying lovemaking was exactly what they needed to make it possible for them to understand each other better.

## *Variety*

Most couples at one time or another will reach the conclusion that their sex life would be improved by adding a little
"variety," meaning anything from joining a swingers group to
having sex in the shower occasionally. Definitions of *variety*
vary widely from couple to couple and—here's where the
trouble comes in—from one partner to the other. Inhibitions
keep many people from enjoying sexual variety. Differences
between partners in the need for variety can create problems.

Some typical ways of adding variety to sex include more
frequent, varied, and prolonged episodes of oral sex; anal sex;
use of sex toys, videos, costumes, and props; sex games and
role-playing, like bondage, light S/M, erotic spanking and fantasy play-acting; and mutual masturbation.

1. Do you feel as though your sex life could be described
   as "routine"?
2. Does your partner feel that way?
3. Is oral stimulation part of your sex life?
4. Have you experimented with sexual variations, such as
   anal sex, spanking, bondage, or S/M?
5. Do you and your partner share your fantasies?
6. Would you feel threatened if your partner suggested
   doing something together you'd never done before?

### The Examples

*The Midlife Panic*

Lee, fifty-eight, complained that sex with his wife, Ruth,
fifty-five, was "routine and mundane." "I need variety," he
said. Lee had introduced sex toys into their lovemaking; and

Ruth had accepted that, but she balked at acting out S/M fantasies or visiting a swinging club. "He makes me feel like I have to do these things to prove my love," Ruth said. "I don't think we need to play with whips or have sex with other couples. I enjoy sex in a variety of positions. We have a lot of oral sex. I am happy to masturbate for him. But I am content with stopping there."

For personal reasons rooted in his life experiences before he met Ruth, Lee felt an urgency in middle age to experience everything he thought he'd missed, including "the ultimate in sexual experiences," before it was too late. Ruth was uncomfortable with some of his suggestions, especially visiting a swinging club. "He's becoming demanding and insensitive," she said. "I don't want to feel like I have to go along with him or he'll go without me."

It's not unusual for middle-aged men to respond to the changes in their sexual functioning with an avid desire for new experiences. The new is more arousing than the familiar, providing a reassuring measure of firmness to an erection. Some men take that quest to limits their partners find too extreme.

### The Inhibited Partner

"When he says he wants more variety, he just means he wants more fellatio," Jean, thirty-three, complained. According to her husband, Ernie, thirty-nine, they'd been having the same oral sex fight for ten years. "I like to perform cunnilingus, too," he said in his own defense. "She doesn't want oral sex for her benefit either." Jean thought sex was fine "without that."

She protested that cunnilingus did nothing for her while

fellatio hurt her jaw. When pressed, she admitted that she believed oral stimulation was "dirty" and "not normal sex." Often women, and men, too, refuse to vary from a sexual routine because they have inhibitions and defend them by labeling sex practices they fear as "dirty" or "abnormal." That stance makes the partner assume the role of "pervert" and relieves the inhibited one of guilt.

### The Inexperienced Couple

Lilly and Bob, both in their mid-twenties, had been together two years when they came into the office. "We have a good sex life," Lilly said; and Bob agreed. But he added, "I don't understand why she doesn't like to receive manual stimulation. She likes oral stimulation, penetration, and even a vibrator. Why not manual?"

He was particularly concerned because he'd read that women needed manual stimulation in addition to intercourse to reach an orgasm. But Lilly had complex reasons for not allowing herself to find pleasure in that kind of touch. "A woman should be able to come without that," she said. Later she disclosed that she "felt cheap" when he put his fingers against her clitoris or inside her body. She'd been sexually active—though not satisfied—at an early age. In those experiences "boys" had probed her vagina with their fingers. When her husband touched her, she remembered her past "shame and the feelings of being used by boys."

These couples and others like them who resist change in their sex lives can be effectively helped with the 21-Day Passion Fix program. Because the Provocative Encounters are brief, they are less threatening than new experiences typically are. It's easier to face down inhibitions and fears, if you know you only have to do so for ten minutes and not an indefinite period of lovemaking time. The brief encounters enable the resisting partner to meet the other's needs for variety without feeling exploited.

## Frequency and Boredom

Disagreements over how often to have sex are as common as crabgrass. Rare are the partners who are in perfect sexual sync throughout a long relationship. Every couple experiences sexual highs and lows over time. Life events—such as fatigue, job stress, loss of a job, death of a family member, or the birth of a child—can drain passion from one partner or another. A couple may also stop having frequent sex because they have performance problems or unresolved relationship or sexual issues. One may be pushing for sex while the other withdraws.

Sometimes both partners feel as though they aren't having enough sex. Lack of time and lack of energy are the most frequently cited reasons for their sexual malaise. They are less likely to tell each other, "I don't want to have sex because it's become boring," than to say, "Not, tonight, honey, I'm too tired." But boredom with the sexual routine is often the unnamed problem.

1. Are you satisfied with the frequency of lovemaking?
2. Is your partner satisfied with the frequency?
3. Does one partner, more than the other, make excuses for not having sex?
4. Do you often feel that sex has becoming boring?
5. Do you suspect your partner might feel that way?

## The Examples

*The Classic Conflict*

Todd and his wife, Cynthia, a professional couple in their early thirties, couldn't agree on how often to make love. "We only have sex twice a week," he said. "That's not enough. I'm always begging her for sex. And I'm tired of feeling rejected." She said, "I'm satisfied with sex twice a week. We don't have time for more sex right now. I'm as tired of his begging for sex as he is. Sometimes I think he doesn't think about anything else. I feel like an object."

Cynthia didn't understand that Todd was a far less secure person than she was. He needed the validation of lovemaking to feel good about himself and safe in their marriage. People have different emotional and sexual security needs. When the less interested partner understands why the other seems more needy, she or he often becomes more responsive.

*The Sex Avoiders*

Amy, twenty-nine, and Chris, thirty-three, decided they had a problem when neither could remember the last time they'd made love. "I thought it was two weeks," she said, "but he said, 'No, I think it was a month.' We looked at each other and said, 'Uh-oh.'" Chris added, "We got scared. Were we going to turn into one of those couples who had a business arrangement and a parenting partnership, not a marriage?"

Following the birth of their son two years earlier, Chris and Amy moved across the country for his job. She had to find a new job. "While we were getting settled in our jobs, finding a house and a nanny, and generally trying to cope with all the adjustments, we drifted apart sexually," Amy said. "When we

24

did make love, it wasn't exciting."

Chris finally acknowledged that he felt their sex life was "boring." Amy, too, conceded that it was. "But that's a function of having so little time," she said. "No time for improvisation."

Many couples believe that good sex has to take a long time. They avoid making love when they don't have a lot of time because they fear she won't have an orgasm. Men don't want to leave their partners feeling frustrated and disappointed anymore than the women want to be left in that position. But sex doesn't have to be an either/or proposition: Either lovemaking is prolonged or it isn't satisfying, especially for her. Provocative Encounters challenge that old assumption.

## *Initiating Sex*

Who initiates sexually in a relationship often reveals the couple dynamics. Inequality in initiating can indicate a pattern of control that extends to other aspects of the relationship. Typically the partner who more often initiates the sex takes more control in general. But that's not always true. In some relationships, the passive partner exerts his or her dominance by rejecting overtures. Some initiating partners complain that they don't feel truly desired by their mates. Equal sex partners are often equal in other aspects of their relationship as well.

1. Do you initiate sex more often or does your partner?
2. If you rarely initiate sex, do you often reject your partner's advances?

3. Do you feel hurt if you initiate sex and your partner isn't interested?

4. Does your partner sometimes say that she or he feels undesirable because you never initiate sex?

## The Examples

### The Leading Man

Paul, a successful businessman in his late forties, is accustomed to making decisions and taking charge in all areas of his life, including his marriage. Susan, thirty-nine, stays at home with their young children and lets him be her leading man. "I always initiate sex," Paul said. "If I didn't, we would never have sex. I want her to be more interested in making love to me than she is." Susan said, "I love his strength. Sometimes I wish I had more power in our marriage, but I do like being a full-time mother. That has made me dependent. I can't switch gears and come on to him in the bedroom when I do what he wants everywhere else." She added, "I never say no to him."

Susan thought that by never saying no, she was giving Paul everything he needed and wanted from her sexually. In the early days of their marriage, Paul was happy with her acquiescence. But he had begun questioning her desire for him. In counseling, he admitted that he resented the burden of authority in the relationship. He wanted her to take more responsibility for decision-making—and especially for their sex life.

Domineering men often do reach that point in their marriages. They are tired of being in charge. And they begin to resent the female passivity they once found erotic. Suddenly he wants her to switch gears; and she is confused.

## The Rejecting Partner

Larry, thirty-one, and Renee, thirty, came into the office because, after three years of marriage, they had stopped having sex. "I quit asking her," he said. "She always refused me. After we hadn't done it for a few months, she asked me what was wrong. It took her a long time to notice, didn't it? But, even after she realized I'd stopped asking, she didn't ask." Renee countered that Larry "pressured me so much about sex I felt backed into a corner. Then suddenly he lost interest. I think he's having an affair."

Once Larry convinced her that he wasn't having an affair, Renee initiated sex occasionally—but not often. Larry didn't initiate either. His sexual desire diminished as his confidence plummeted. When her overtures weren't met with him asking her the next time, Renee felt rejected, too. Their sexual insecurities and unacknowledged power issues were strangling their desire.

Men and women who are insecure in their sexuality tend to withdraw when they feel rejected. Their withdrawal reinforces the passive partner's position. Both become unwilling to take a risk; and no one initiates lovemaking.

The 21-Day Passion Fix program takes the pressure off both partners. They agree to do three Provocative Encounters each week. Who initiates is no longer an issue blocking their sexual expression.

## Orgasms

Difficulty in reaching orgasm is more often a woman's problem than a man's. But in relationships, men take on the burden of responsibility—and guilt!—when a woman doesn't reach orgasm. The common male problem is rapid ejaculation, or reaching orgasm too quickly. Occasionally a man may suffer from an inability to reach orgasm, called "retarded ejaculation." Obviously orgasm difficulties, either hers or his, are relationship problems, too.

Emotional and psychological issues can short-circuit the orgasmic process. Women or men who fear the sense of letting go that accompanies orgasm or who feel distrustful of their partners may not be able to reach climax, no matter what the partner does. But orgasm often doesn't occur in women because they aren't getting the kind of stimulation they need. The majority of women—approximately two-thirds of all women—need direct clitoral stimulation, the kind they probably don't get through intercourse alone, to reach orgasm. Technique is also an issue here.

1.  Are you orgasmic in most of your sexual encounters?
2.  Is your partner orgasmic in most of your sexual encounters?
3.  Do you feel you could be more orgasmic if your partner changed his or her lovemaking style or learned new techniques?
4.  Have you ever avoided lovemaking because orgasm—his or hers—was an issue or a problem?

**The Examples**
*The Anorgasmic Woman*
Lisa, fifty-five, claimed that Todd, forty-five, her new husband, was a "wonderful lover." She said, "I adore him; and our

life together is perfect." Well, not quite. A skillful lover, Todd realized that Lisa was not having orgasms even when she more or less pretended she was. "I'm not satisfying her," he said. "This really bothers me." Lisa insisted, "I am satisfied with our sexual relationship. I don't need to have an orgasm to enjoy sex."

Soon Lisa confessed that she'd never experienced an orgasm with a partner, though she was orgasmic via masturbation. In lovemaking, Lisa became highly excited, especially in her lovemaking with Todd, but she always "shut down," both physically and emotionally before reaching orgasm. "I feel myself getting to the same high point every time," she said. "Then I pull back."

Although Lisa trusted her husband, she had a history of relationships with men who disappointed her. Shutting down, or pulling back, had become her sexual habit. Once she recognized that she was emotionally blocking orgasm, she was motivated to change her behavior. Together she and Todd experimented with different types of mental and physical stimulation until she eventually reached orgasm with her husband.

### The Premature Male

Rachel, thirty-seven, and Burt, twenty-eight, both have high sex drives. "I thought we were compatible," she said. "Then we got married." After six months together, they were enmeshed in a lovemaking pattern that wasn't satisfactory to either one. Because both traveled in their jobs, they were together only two or three nights a week. The sex was intense, but all too brief. "He comes before I get started," Rachel complained. Burt blamed their schedules for leaving him "desperately horny every time we get together." He claimed, "If we had sex more often, I wouldn't orgasm so quickly when we do make love."

Upon closer examination, Rachel and Burt recognized that rapid ejaculation had always been a problem for him. During their courtship, they had time for prolonged love-making sessions—in which he was able to get erect again after his quick ejaculation, continue making love, and climax again. A man's ability to rejuvenate in less than thirty minutes diminishes rapidly as he moves through his twenties. If travel hadn't transformed their sexual behavior, the normal aging process would have. Together they learned some simple techniques for delaying his ejaculation.

In some men, rapid ejaculation and certainly retarded ejaculation are problems with their roots in emotional or psychological issues. But, for many men like Burt, rapid ejaculation is a technical problem that can be fairly easily cured. Both men and women need to reach orgasm and have their partners reach orgasm during lovemaking.

Some women maintain that "it doesn't matter" if they reach orgasm. It does matter. A woman doesn't have to reach orgasm every time she makes love, but she needs to have an orgasm often enough to feel satisfied with her sex life. Orgasm intensifies the physical, emotional, and psychological feelings of lovemaking—and validates the lover, too.

## Do You Know Where You Are?

Now that you've both answered the questions, you should have a much better understanding of the strengths and weaknesses of your sexual relationship. Maybe you understand why you've let yourselves become too busy, too tired, and too stressed to make love. Some of your answers have likely surprised your partner—and vice versa. Even if you've been together for decades, you've learned something new about each other in the process of answering these questions.

There are probably some differences in what you both want from lovemaking. Those differences are out in the open now. And, you may be ready to compromise so that each partner gets the most important sexual needs met.

You're ready to move on to setting sexual goals. This is going to be fun!

## Chapter 2
## *Setting Sexual Goals*

MOST PEOPLE don't approach their sexual problems the same way they approach problems in other important areas of their lives. The woman who has difficulty asking for cunnilingus is probably not shy about telling her partner she wants him to do his share of the household chores. The man who rejects his wife's advances because he is afraid he can't get or maintain an erection wouldn't let fear of performance failure keep him from learning how to play a better game of golf. And let's be honest: Would "too tired," "too busy," or "not in the mood" get in the way of the pursuit of career and financial goals?

Think about an important goal that you and your partner have achieved together, for example, buying a house, starting a family, or building an investment portfolio. You can use the same basic approach for achieving sexual goals. Ask yourselves:

What steps did we take to reach that goal?
How did we handle differences of opinion about what we wanted or how we should get it?

32

How did we work out compromises so that each of us got
at least part of what we wanted?

Goal setting is simply making a plan, negotiating differences, and measuring progress. The process of working
together toward a goal has benefits to a relationship, even if
the goals aren't fully realized. Couples who set and achieve
goals refine their communication skills and hone their conflict
resolution techniques. Their shared satisfaction and sense of
accomplishment carries over to other areas of the relationship
as well.

People generally work more effectively together when
they can define problems in simple yet concrete terms before
tackling solutions. Here are the basic steps for doing that with
any problem:

1. *Assign a name to the issue without assigning blame.* Give
   each problem a label that both partners understand
   and accept. In other words, the problem isn't, "You
   spend too much on clothes," or "You come too fast
   when we make love"—but *discretionary income spending*
   and *the sexual orgasm phase.*
2. *Translate the negative, the problem, into a plan for creating a
   positive, the goal.* Stop endlessly complaining about
   what's wrong. Brainstorm suggestions for making it
   right. This takes you out of the rut of the hopeless
   predicament. Now you have a working solution.
3. *Break the solution down into workable steps.* Solving a
   problem can seem like an overwhelming task if you
   look at it as one great leap. Don't set yourself up for

failure by expecting to lose twenty pounds in a week or perfecting a new sex technique the first time you try it.

4. *Create a realistic time frame for accomplishing your goal.* A time limit encourages motivation and sustains focus. Otherwise that goal of "exercising" or "making love more often" is added to a long list of things that may never get done, like "cleaning the closets." And for some people change is difficult. They need to have an endpoint in sight.

## The Most Common Sexual Goals

You and your partner will likely find your goals, as determined by your answers to the questionnaire, in this list of sexual goals frequently cited by clients in my practice. Look through the list and see where you fit in. Under each goal, you'll find a set of guidelines for applying the basic goal-setting steps defined in the previous section to your sexual problem. Then I'll give you examples of how real couples were able to translate their problems into plans for solutions. By the end of this chapter, you should have the foundation for starting the 21-Day Passion Fix program, which includes:

- A clear picture of where you are sexually, which you got from answering the questionnaire
- A mutual agreement on where you want to be three weeks from now, which you'll get from setting goals
- An understanding of how to shape Fantasy and Provocative Encounters to achieve those goals

## More Frequent Lovemaking

Sometimes one partner, but often both, wants to make love more often than they do. They have no specific complaints about lovemaking. In fact, they may say, "Sex is fine when we do it." "No time," "too busy," and "too tired" are excuses for not having sex more often. They feel disconnected from each other because they aren't making love often enough.

## Becoming More "Romantic"

Women complain about the lack of romance in their lives. Men are more apt to say the "passion" or the "thrill" is gone. But they're talking about the same problem: An absence or a lack of the tender and urgent words and gestures that make a woman or a man feel desired and appreciated by a partner.

## Increasing Arousal

The sex may seem "boring" or "not as exciting as it was" because one or both partners aren't becoming highly aroused. A woman may not become sufficiently aroused to reach orgasm. Or a man may have difficulty sustaining his arousal— and lose his erection. The sex isn't "hot" anymore.

## Adding Variety or "More Creative" Lovemaking

They make love in more or less the same way all the time. Some couples may have stopped adding variety to their sex lives because they're "too busy" and being creative in bed "takes time." The sameness of their routine leaves both feeling a little dissatisfied. Secretly they fantasize about playing a bondage game or making love in the pool, but they don't share their fantasies with each other.

### More Oral Sex

Men cite this as a goal slightly more often than women do. But a woman often has her first or strongest orgasm via cunnilingus. As couples and/or the relationship ages, oral sex becomes more important, in part because a man may need fellatio to restore a flagging erection.

### Improving Technique

Here's one of the biggest myths about sex: It doesn't matter how you perform fellatio (or cunnilingus or manual stimulation, etc.), it's the thought that counts. Maybe that's true in the beginning when passion conquers all. Later, technique counts.

### Orgasms!

Here's another sex myth: Women don't care about orgasms because they enjoy the "closeness" or "intimacy" of lovemaking without orgasm. Orgasms do matter. A woman may have difficulty reaching orgasm on a regular basis. She may want to experience multiple orgasms. Both men and women may want to have more intense or longer orgasms. Often couples fear they are not having a true peak experience.

## Opening the Lines of Sexual Communication

Most couples have at least some difficulty telling each other what they really want in bed. Typically, they communicate without words or through the use of safe code words and phrases. They would like to learn a better way, but, for some couples, communication is the major problem. Neither knows what the other wants and needs.

# Applying the Goal-Setting Method to Sex Problems

You are reading this book because your sex life needs a tune-up. Sex is not as satisfying as you and your partner would like it to be, probably not as satisfying as you remember it once was. Now you have targeted the problem areas and are ready to identify your sexual goals. This is how you apply the general goal-setting process to your sex life.

## Step 1: Talk

Some people have an easier time talking about sex than others. The key to success: Approach each other in a positive and supportive manner. Let the partner most comfortable talking about sex take the lead. Protect your partner's self-esteem by emphasizing the positive aspects of your sexual experiences together before gently exploring the areas that could be improved.

First, talk about sex in general. Tell your partner how important a specific, and pleasurable, sexual experience was to you. When you both feel comfortable, discuss the question-naire and your answers. Have the questionnaires in front of you because the presence of paperwork makes conversation easier, if for no other reason than it gives you something to do with your hands and your eyes when you're nervous. Identify specific sexual patterns that your answers have made obvious; for example, one partner's complaint that there is no time for sex or another's dissatisfaction with the lack of variety or oral sex in lovemaking.

Elicit comments from your partner by asking questions. Were you surprised by each other's answers? What are the areas of agreement and disagreement? What area clearly needs attention first?

Having a frank discussion in which you both can be vul-nerable increases the intimate connection immediately. *Example:* Marie felt awkward and self-conscious talking about sex. She used vague general terms, describing their sex life as "generally fine." Tony, who was eager to talk about sex in spe-cific terms, was the leader in their discussion. He asked the questions and gently elicited her answers. By the time they'd finished the questionnaire, she was able to speak more candidly.

### Step 2: Make Two Lists

Drawing upon the questionnaire answers and the discus-sion, each of you should make a list of ways in which you would like to improve your sex life. The list should be no longer than eight points. Longer lists seem overwhelming, both to the list maker and the partner. Prioritize the list by put-ting the most important concerns first and concluding with those areas in which you're willing to compromise. Maybe, for example, you would like to make love in the shower—item 8—but you urgently want, even need, to have sex more often, making "increase frequency" your first priority.

Can you group together some of your points to simplify the list? For example, "more variety" and "increase sexual creativity" are linked. "More oral sex" and "improve oral technique, including kissing" also belong together.

*Example:* Mary had tried to talk to Joe about her sexual dissatisfaction, but she typically became too emotional to focus on the subject in a positive, helpful way. Making a list helped her feel more prepared for a discussion. Joe was more comfortable with initially writing his sexual goals than talking about them, too. They both felt less overwhelmed by the idea of improving their sex life after they took pen in hand.

### Step 3: Integrate Your Lists

Share your lists. Look first for the areas of agreement; for example, you both want "to make more time for sex," "to increase arousal," and "to add romance" to your life. Make one unified list of these common sexual goals. Prioritize that list as you did your individual lists. Doing this will be easier if you both feel heard, respected, and understood.

Making the list together shouldn't be an excuse for rehashing old arguments about when, how, and how often to have sex. Consider this your opportunity to take a fresh look at some old issues. The 21-Day Passion Fix program will help you work out bedroom conflicts that have gone unresolved, even unspoken, for years.

And, you don't have to negotiate a time frame. That's done for you. In three weeks, you will have reached your goals.

*Example:* Steve and Anne had trouble combining their lists. At first glance, Anne didn't like his goals. She considered them threatening. Steve wanted her to be more sexually aggressive and to act out some of his fantasies. After a long discussion, each agreed to give some ground to the other. Anne would try to be more expressive sexually if Steve would agree that the fantasies they shared would be very romantic ones.

## Step 4: Establish Your Criteria for Success

Sex isn't a science experiment; and success can be a subjective event. How do you know whether your goals have been met? If the goal is "increase arousal," for example, he may feel successful if he prolongs intercourse before ejaculation while she may be disappointed that she hasn't reached a higher level of arousal, even if she had an orgasm.

Agree on some form of measurable criteria. The 21-Day Passion Fix program will help you do that naturally by requiring you to have one Fantasy Encounter and three Provocative Encounters each week. That requirement takes care of increasing frequency and other likely goals, such as including more creativity and variety in lovemaking. Also there is a short evaluation quiz at the end of each week.

*Example:* Ben and Abby debated over the meaning of success without coming up with a definition that pleased both of them. Finally, she suggested: Simplify. They agreed that they would introduce one new sexual position and one new sex toy each week—with the understanding that they would drop the position or the toy from their repertoire if either failed to be aroused or satisfied.

## What If You Still Can't Agree on Sexual Goals?

Don't be discouraged. Many couples find this first hurdle the most difficult. There are several reasons that creating common goals in this intimate area of life can be challenging:

1. Many couples have fallen into the habit of making too many negative statements about their sex life. "You never want to give me oral sex." "I never get an orgasm." "You always rush." "You're never in the mood." They don't know how to talk in a positive way, being supportive and encouraging of one another. Their individual goals list may be more about what their partner does wrong than what they would like to do together to make things better.

2. Some couples are used to pretending everything is "basically okay," when it isn't. For them, admitting that they are dissatisfied seems threatening to the safe status quo. Their lists may not be as specific as they need to be.

3. Fears and inhibitions may keep some men and women from integrating their partner's list into their own. Maybe he's afraid he won't be able to perform up to her standards. Or she doesn't know how to overcome her inhibitions about certain sex acts. They will fiercely protect their own priorities rather than consider the other's.

Here's how even the most stubborn individuals can learn how to mesh their sexual goals as a couple:

1. *Listen.* Hear and try to understand the other's perspective, even if you don't agree with it. People feel better when they know they've been heard. Listening shows respect. It validates your partner without necessarily indicating agreement. When you really listen, you may hear something that you hadn't heard before. You may discover your partner's vulnerability.
2. *Ask questions.* Don't say, "No, I can't; I won't." Ask, "Why does this appeal to you? Why do you feel this way? What do you mean when you say this?" Taking the discussion past "I want" and "I don't want" opens doors.
3. *Agree to fantasize your differences.* If one partner wants a sexual activity the other finds distasteful, work out a fantasy compromise. Agree to talk about that sex act while doing another one. The Fantasy Encounter is the ideal place for the acts one partner may consider "taboo" in real life.
4. *Practice the golden "quid pro quo" rule.* Give something to get something. She wants to make love with rose petals on the bed; and he wants her to talk dirty to him. Sometimes she gets rose petals; and sometimes he gets the dirty talk.

## How Some Couples Developed Their Sexual Goals

These short examples from my practice might inspire you if you're having trouble identifying and setting sexual goals.

## *More Frequent Lovemaking*

No matter what their other goals may be, most couples in my practice come into the office initially because they are suffering from low—or no—sexual desire. Many are working parents of toddler or school-age children. Overwhelmed by responsibilities and demands on their time, they have become accustomed to putting sex last. Unconsciously suppressing desire, they focus on duties and responsibilities. When they have time for sex, they have little desire, a natural consequence of suppressing it.

Dave and Linda are typical partners worried about their lack of desire. Initially he didn't identify the demands of their hectic schedules as a problem. He thought her difficulty in becoming sufficiently aroused to reach orgasm was the problem.

"She has trouble reaching orgasm," Dave said, "so we put off having sex until we had an hour for seduction, foreplay, and cunnilingus before intercourse. Finding an hour doesn't happen often enough for me. I'm frustrated."

Because Dave was frustrated, he couldn't focus on her complaints: not enough romance, low desire, insufficient arousal. His primary goal was "more sex, especially more oral sex," while hers was "more romance."

They saw how their goals meshed when they acknowledged that they both needed to reorganize their priorities. On their common goal list, number one was "make more time for sex." She realized that having sex more often would make him more predisposed to romantic behavior.

## *Becoming More Romantic*

Larry was adamant that *romance* and *sex* were separate issues. He wanted more sex; Tina wanted more romance. But what, he asked, did that have to do with sex? Tina was equally adamant in her position: Good sex begins outside the bedroom. She won him over by promising to dress "sexier" at home. His eyes lit up at the prospect of seeing his wife in the kind of clothing she'd worn when they were dating. He also agreed to take more trouble with his appearance on weekends, something he would never have identified as a sexual goal.

Before their first Provocative Encounter, Tina bought some attractive casual outfits to replace her ubiquitous sweats and threw out the old shirts she wore to bed. He promised to shave on weekends, be more affectionate outside the bedroom, and bring her flowers. Women need affection and romantic attention to maintain sexual desire for their spouses. Once Larry identified that kind of behavior as a necessary form of foreplay, he had no trouble making "romance" a priority goal.

## *Increasing Arousal*

Stan and Susan acknowledged they were awkward as lovers. Insecurity and personal feelings of inadequacy had kept them from exploring their own and each other's erotic natures. They didn't really know how to arouse each other. So they identified their problem simply as "boring sex" because they didn't understand that neither was particularly aroused during lovemaking.

Their mutual goal was to make sex more exciting. Susan thought Stan should figure out how to do that. He resented her lack of input. Finally, they purchased instructional videos to give them some ideas. She was the first to recognize their real problem: insufficient arousal. They agreed to experiment with different types of stimulation and intercourse positions to increase arousal.

## Adding Variety or More Creative Lovemaking

Bonnie and Stuart agreed that a big problem in their sexual relationship was lack of variety. For the duration of their twelve-year marriage, they'd been making love the same way. Their pattern was a classic: some kissing, caressing, and manual and oral foreplay, followed by intercourse in the missionary position. While they both knew they were stuck in a rut, they couldn't agree on how to climb out of it.

Their sexual goal-setting process was short-circuited by Bonnie's reluctance to experiment. She labeled sex toys "unnatural" and rejected any intercourse position she considered "too gymnastic," including the female superior position. But she wanted Stuart to devote more time to manual stimulation of her clitoris during intercourse, something he had for the most part failed to do. They were able to reach a consensus on goals when he agreed to satisfy her desire for manual stimulation if she would try out one new position, oral technique, or sex toy per week.

## More Oral Sex

Marcy and Jack, like many couples, had been arguing about oral sex for a long time. But their argument had a slightly different spin. In the most common scenario, the man wants more fellatio than the woman likes to give or the woman wants more cunnilingus than the man is willing to give. Sometimes inhibitions stop couples from enjoying or performing oral sex. Marcy loved oral sex, the giving and the receiving of it. She enjoyed cunnilingus immensely and experienced satisfying orgasms this way. But Jack claimed that fellatio did little for him, leaving Marcy feeling inadequate in sexually pleasing Jack.

Her goal was "more oral sex." His goal was "better technique." When he set that goal, he didn't realize she already felt incompetent at oral sex. Fortunately, he was able to save the situation by praising other aspects of her lovemaking, like her responsiveness. They developed a shared goal: She would experiment with new fellatio techniques and learn how to arouse Jack orally. They accomplished their goal! Jack became more aroused by fellatio than he'd dreamed possible; and Marcy gained a lot of sexual confidence from being able to do that.

### Improving Technique

Technique was the major problem for Bob and Lois. But their underlying difficulty was inexperience, exacerbated by inhibitions. She came from a strict religious family. He had an unhappy, and not very sexual, early marriage that ended in divorce when his wife left him for another man. Both were unskilled lovers. Unrealistic expectations and unshared fantasies compounded their problem. Bob said their primary goal was "more sex." Lois said it was "for him to kiss me without slobbering all over me."

Bob was shocked to learn she didn't like his kisses. But that did, he conceded, begin to explain why Lois never wanted sex. He wasn't exciting her in the most basic way. They agreed to make "improving communication" and "improving love-making techniques" their major goals. Lois told him how she liked to be kissed. Then she actually took charge of the kissing and showed him how to do it. They moved from kissing to touching, caressing, and manually and orally stimulating each other. As they became more skillful at arousing and pleasing each other, they shared fantasies. Each was surprised to discover a passionate partner.

### Orgasms!

Alan was surprised when Joan confessed she found sex "tedious, more often than not." Why was she bored by love-making? Joan rarely had an orgasm, though she often faked one "to end the sex." When asked why had she faked so often, Joan replied, "To spare his feelings, because he tries to please me." Understandably, Alan felt angry and betrayed. But he did acknowledge later that he had often suspected her of faking. "You don't get excited enough," he told her. Alan was determined to make exciting her to the point of orgasm more often their number one goal, but she balked. She didn't think they should "work so hard" to give her an orgasm.

Finally Alan agreed to a concession. He wouldn't treat giving her an orgasm as a goal, if she would agree to expand their sexual repertoire to include more oral sex, more frequent lovemaking, whether or not that included intercourse, and more creativity. He wanted to act out fantasies. She didn't mind doing that as long as the focus of every sexual encounter wasn't her orgasm.

As often happens when the pressure is reduced and new lovemaking tactics are employed, Joan became more orgasmic anyway.

## Opening the Lines of Sexual Communication

Some couples have difficulty talking about sex at all. Patty and Charlie were able to communicate fairly well as long as they were asking, "Would you like to make love tonight?" or saying, "A little more to the left . . . yes, that's it!" But they had never told each other their hidden desires or shared sexual secrets like her admitting she was aroused by pornography. No wonder they were increasingly "too busy" for lovemaking, which both labeled "fairly routine."

Patty shocked Charlie when she listed "talk dirty" as a sexual goal. She found the idea of dirty talk highly arousing and provocative. He didn't want to hear his wife say "words like that in bed" nor did he want to say them to her. Charlie had a surprising goal of his own: He wanted to dabble in role-playing, especially bondage games. "I fantasize tying Patty to the bed and having my way with her," he said. She didn't like the idea.

At first they thought their goals were divergent. They began to explore ways of incorporating her wish—dirty talk—and his wish—fantasy games and bondage—into their lovemaking. The more they talked, the more open each felt to fulfilling the other's desires. They devised compromises suitable to both.

He agreed to say specific words that excited her while she was tied up, using Velcro restraints so she would feel as though she could escape. She promised to speak her dialogue in a soft, sexy voice that he found appealing. Patty was surprised to discover how much she enjoyed fulfilling his fantasy.

His aggressive and dominating behavior in bed excited her as much as it did him. And she enjoyed surrendering control of the lovemaking to him occasionally, especially since she got to speak and hear those thrilling words. Without the questionnaire to inspire their intimate communication, neither would have told the other about their secret desires.

## *Are You Ready for Your Passion Fix?*

If you've completed the work in these two chapters, you are ready to design the Fantasy and Provocative Encounters that will dramatically improve your sex life in twenty-one days. The sexual problems and issues you've defined and the goals you've established will influence your choices of Fantasy Encounter scenarios—and later, Provocative Encounters. Remember that activities one partner finds unpleasant or threatening as physical encounters can be woven into the Fantasy Encounters.

The next chapter outlines the 21-Day Passion Fix program in easy-to-follow steps. Subsequent chapters will show you how to develop your encounters. You'll be given a checklist after every one of those chapters to measure your progress toward achieving your goals.

In working with hundreds of couples in this program, I've

never had a "failure." Every couple who has followed the guidelines of the 21-Day Passion Fix program has reported at least some measure of success. At the end of three weeks, they are having sex more often. And, they are having better sex.

Are you ready for your relationship Passion Fix?

# PART TWO

# THE 21-DAY PASSION FIX PROGRAM

*Chapter 3*
## How—and Why—
## the Passion Fix Program Works

WHAT'S THE FIRST THING to go when one or both partners are busy, tired, or stressed?

*Sex.* The chores somehow get done. The scheduling demands are met. And work, family, and homeowner responsibilities are more or less covered. But, there's no time or energy left for sex.

How do many couples handle sexual inhibitions or insecurities?

*They avoid having sex.* He won't ask her why she doesn't want him to perform cunnilingus or make love to her in the shower. He'll just assume his lovemaking disappoints her—and he'll avoid disappointing her often by seldom initiating sex. Or, if he's avoiding her because he fears losing his erection during lovemaking, she won't blame his insecurity. She'll think, "He doesn't find me sexy anymore."

What do couples do when they have difficulty talking about a sex problem?

*They avoid having sex.* Avoidance seems like a safe haven to men and women who don't know how to talk about sex. A frank discussion is a threatening prospect.

How do couples handle one partner's performance problem? Or lack of lovemaking skills?

*They avoid having sex.* These couples also say they are too tired, too busy, too stressed, or have no time for sex. But they're really afraid of disappointing or hurting their partner. They don't know how to deal with performance or technique issues.

How do couples cope with devastating personal and relationship problems?

Often, *they stop having sex*—just when they need intimacy the most. Maybe they're tired and have no energy in part because they don't have sex. Lovemaking can revitalize and restore men and women. Sex isn't depleting. It's energizing.

Whether lack of time and energy are the causes or the symptoms and excuses, they are the reasons most couples give for not making love. The end result is the same: The couple has sex seldom, rarely, or, at least "not often enough."

As the habit of avoidance grows, many couples find themselves growing more tired, not less. They may be getting that extra fifteen minutes of sleep they gained by not having sex, but they have less and less energy. They complain they have no personal time to be romantic with each other or to think and plan for lovemaking.

Couples often treat lovemaking as a luxury they can't afford until something makes them realize their relationship is suffering from the lack of it. Then they feel guilty about not having enough sex. A woman may say she's "cheating" her partner out of the lovemaking "he deserves." A man may fear his wife is losing her sexual confidence because he rarely desires her. They feel guilty about not giving each other more pleasure. And they feel insecure because they are not the sizzling sex partners exemplified in popular novels, magazine articles, and movies.

Though couples with unsatisfying sex lives represent a diverse group of people who have many different underlying problems—one partner in each couple will almost always say, "We would have sex more often, but there just never seems to be enough time."

## Who Are the "No Time, No Energy, No Desire" Couples?

These couples are different in many ways, but they all have something in common: They seldom have sex. And, they're adept at rationalizing the lack of lovemaking in their lives, too. Who are the No Time, No Energy couples?

Almost every couple at some point in their lives together will fall into that category for a while, for example, after the birth of a child, a promotion into a demanding job, the launching of a new business enterprise, an illness, or a loss within the nuclear or extended family. In other cases, the lack of time and energy are excuses, covering other problems or issues.

These couples are:

- *The workers.* Both are probably working and also likely the parents of young or school-age children. One may

54

still be attending college or working on an advanced degree. They live by the time dictates of their crammed schedules. And "sex" doesn't make the appointment book.

- *The inexperienced or inadequate lover(s).* She or he avoids sex out of embarrassment or fear of repeating another bad lovemaking experience and doesn't know how to acquire sexual technique skills. "Busy" or "tired" make acceptable excuses.

- *Couples who have communication issues in general, specifically sexual communication issues.* They don't know how to talk about what's wrong with their sex lives without hurting each other's feelings. They aren't able to articulate their desires.

- *Men, and women, who suffer from sexual performance anxiety.* He has difficulty achieving or maintaining an erection. She reaches orgasm infrequently if at all.

- *Couples who have let their sexual differences about how, when, and how often to make love create a sexual stalemate.* Some couples almost stop making love because, for example, one or the other refuses to perform oral sex. In many cases, control is the real issue. One partner says no to sex as a means of attaining power in the relationship.

- *Partners who let unresolved anger and other underlying marital issues simmer beneath the surface of their relationship.* One or both don't feel heard, appreciated, understood, or important. Desire fades in an unappreciated partner.

- *Men and women who never found their mate physically or sexually attractive.* They married for financial security or to have a family with someone they considered a good parenting prospect. Desire was low in the beginning. Now that they are busy as parents and providers, they have no desire.

- *Couples who have lost the strong emotional and sexual connection they once had.* Maybe they've experienced serious financial, career, or family difficulties that have left them feeling isolated from each other and emotionally depleted. One or both may have had an affair.

- *Men and women who have stopped paying attention to their appearance.* One may have gained a lot of weight, which the partner finds unattractive. Women particularly, but men, too, may add pounds or let their appearance deteriorate to avoid having sex that isn't satisfying. One partner may suffer from deep sexual inhibitions, perhaps rooted in negative childhood messages about sex, and find hiding behind an unattractive façade a comfortable way of avoiding lovemaking.

Abstinence becomes a habit. Couples who put sex off until "later" discover "later" seldom arrives. The typical "no time" couple may connect sexually two or three times a month, even less. Some can't remember when they last made love.

## *How Can Their Sex Life Be Restored?*

These couples need a quick, easy way to reconnect sexually. The "quick" part of that equation can't be emphasized enough. Most sex therapy programs fail because they simply take too much time and require a level of sexual activity that seems unattainable. To become sexually active again, couples who aren't making love on a regular, mutually satisfying basis need a focused goal-oriented program composed of short steps that results in immediate progress.

The 21-Day Passion Fix program, based on Quickies, or Provocative Encounters, was a natural outgrowth of my work with clients who not only didn't have the time for a lengthy program of therapy but also would have felt overwhelmed or intimidated at being handed a prescription for prolonged lovemaking sessions. If a working couple with children and no real sex problems except depleted desire and low energy are daunted by the prospect of taking a course in Tantric love-making or making a romantic new beginning by going out on dates together, imagine how the couple with performance anxieties or hidden relationship issues respond to those suggestions! Their anxieties are at fever pitch; they might try to follow the prescription and "fail." Or they might simply give up on improving their sex life altogether.

If sex has become problematical for whatever reason, planning a weekend hotel getaway where the pressure is on to perform and enjoy is not really the best solution to the problem. That weekend trip might be a satisfying sexual interlude for some couples. But when they get back home, they fall immediately into the same habits that left them feeling sexually deprived.

Couples need a way to rediscover their desire for each other at home in their everyday lives. If they can't do that, sex will become an occasional event, reserved for holiday weekends and summer vacations—*maybe*. Good, satisfying lovemaking has to be incorporated into the schedule. Who wants sex to be the erotic equivalent of decorating the Christmas tree, lighting the menorah, or celebrating Diwali (the Hindu Festival of Lights)?

Getting back into regular lovemaking can be particularly difficult for couples who are avoiding sex because they're really avoiding sex problems. They want a program that will reduce the pressure and be fun, nonthreatening, and easy to follow with immediate benefits for both partners. And they also need a way to handle their performance problems, improve sexual technique, and deal with individual and relationship sexual issues—all within the confines of a program that doesn't make either or both of them feel like a patient in long-term therapy.

The 21-Day Passion Fix program works for every couple, no matter their level of sexual expertise or the scope of their dissatisfaction. Although couples described in this book are primarily in their twenties to fifties, couples in their sixties and up who may be less busy than the no time couples, will find this program immensely helpful. They benefit whether they've been together a few months or twenty or thirty years or more. Why? Because of the program's emphasis on sexual pleasure, not performance, variety, and skill development, mutually arousing fantasies, and short intense passion fixes to increase sexual desire and arousal. The program jump-starts any stalled sex life in one hour per week over a three-week period. The "homework assignments" are brief, but hot—even sizzling. Couples can easily measure their progress because goals and expectations are carefully and clearly laid out in small increments. The 21-Day Passion Fix program helps couples design a sexual environment tailored to their needs and desires.

Satisfaction guaranteed.

## *But, Still You Ask, Why Quickies?*

Quickies have gotten a bad rap among women. Provocative Encounters are not like your grandmother's quickie, a "lie back and submit to intercourse" experience meant to gratify his needs and assuage her conscience that she'd done right by her man. This is not the "wham-bam-thank you, ma'am" sex that you might fear it is. The old quickie was as limiting for him as it was for her. How good could he have felt about himself pumping away in the missionary position trying to get it over fast because he knew the woman beneath him found this marital chore about as thrilling as picking up his socks?

Provocative Encounters are brief, intense pleasure oriented sexual events, sometimes designed to meet her sexual needs, sometimes his, but most often to satisfy both partners. The Encounters may include intercourse or may be limited to manual and oral stimulation. The first and longest encounter, the Fantasy Encounter, is a completely new sexual experience for most couples. It's a no-hands, no-demands form of mental foreplay meant to encourage arousal and spark creativity in lovemaking.

## *Why the New Quickies Now?*

People have never felt more pressed for time in their personal lives than they do at the beginning of the twenty-first century. Time is a factor in most modern marriages and other long-term relationships. Even if you enjoy having sex with your partner, and the sex is generally good, you have likely complained about not having "enough time" to enjoy "good sex." Although long, leisurely lovemaking is a wonderful experience, it's not the only way to make love. If you limit sex to those days and nights when you have the luxury of time, you're missing a lot.

The concept of the brief, intense erotic encounter appealed to the clients in my practice as soon as they grasped its meaning. More important, these encounters were successful with a wide range of clients, from the stressed couple with low desire to a couple with a history of erectile failure and difficulty reaching orgasm. The program works. And, judging from the testimonials of my clients, the significant gains are emotional as well as sexual.

"When our sex life improved, so did our marriage," one male client told me. His wife agreed that they found each other "less irritating than they had in the days of infrequent and not thrilling sex." Make the sex better and you make the relationship better, too.

You can dramatically improve your sex life *quickly*. Isn't that worth doing?

## The 21-Day Passion Fix Program

Before couples begin the program, they fill out the question-naires and establish their mutual sexual goals. In other words, they cover the ground that you have covered in Chapters 1 and 2. You've already completed the hard work. In doing the analysis and goal setting, you've thrown open all the doors and windows in your sexual house and let the air and light flow through. You know what you enjoy about lovemaking and what you want to change. Now you're ready to have fun together.

## The Program

The 21-Day Passion Fix program requires a commitment from each partner to be sexually intimate for at least one hour total per week in a series of prescribed Provocative Encounters. Here's how it's set up:

- The first encounter, the Fantasy Encounter, lasts thirty minutes.
- The three Provocative Encounters last ten minutes each.
- At the end of each week, partners answer seven questions together to evaluate their progress toward meeting their sexual goals.

## Elements of the Fantasy Encounter

Why start with a Fantasy Encounter? It's the natural place to begin.

You've heard it said many times: Sex begins in the brain. A cliché? Yes, but it's still true. Too often busy men and women repress or ignore their sexual thoughts and urges. Rather than enjoying a brief erotic mental interlude fantasizing what that woman on the train looks like naked or how that rugged construction worker might kiss, they censor their thoughts. I don't have the time to fantasize about making love. Or, I'm working now; I shouldn't be thinking about being ravished on a desert island. Or, I shouldn't speculate about what that man/woman would be like in bed because I'm married. Those sexual thoughts and fantasies are not a waste of time or a betrayal of the intimate bond.

But they can be more than stolen solitary pleasures. Think of fantasies as instant and powerful aphrodisiacs. Many people are too inhibited, guilty, or confused about what their fantasies mean to take advantage of them as the natural sexual stimulants they are. A fantasy about someone other than your partner or about a sex act you wouldn't commit can wake up libido—and make you sexier for the one you're with.

That everyone has sexual fantasies is a well-documented fact. Researchers now believe that women have nearly as many fantasies as men and were simply under-reporting their erotic daydreams way back in the 1950s when they said they didn't have them. A decade ago, Nancy Friday reported the then-startling news in her book *Women on Top* that women's fantasies had become more graphic and overtly sexual and aggressive since she first studied them in the 1970s. We all fantasize. Our fantasies are not always about true love and roses. And that's good!

The Fantasy Encounter stimulates this natural talent that is latent in all of us. That's why it is the first activity of the week. Its purpose is to excite desire, very likely a higher level of desire than either partner has felt in a long time. The Fantasy Encounter is mental foreplay for the Provocative Encounters to come.

### Here's How It Works

Set aside thirty minutes of uninterrupted time on Sunday. Wear comfortable but attractive clothes. Sit down together and talk about sexual fantasies, but not necessarily your own fantasies. Many people find sharing fantasies with their partner difficult, even impossibly threatening. Telling him that she fantasizes about his best friend or telling her that he sometimes has violent sexual fantasies—both are normal fantasies—may not be a good way to start the program. Use videos or books for ideas. The goal is to arouse desire in both partners, not to stir up uncomfortable feelings like jealousy and fear.

About twenty minutes into the Encounter, create a mutual fantasy, based on your sexual goals. The fantasy should be arousing to you both. If, for example, "more oral sex" is a primary goal, then the Fantasy Encounter will have an oral sex theme. (The next set of chapters will tell you how to shape that Fantasy Encounter and provide models and examples as well as tips for overcoming any obstacles.) Work out the details like two screenwriters plotting the script for an erotic film. Remember that the fantasy is a good place for adding sexual props, toys, inventive positions, and sex acts that one partner wants to try, but the other doesn't—for example, anal sex.

In doing this exercise, you *must* refrain from any sexual or physical contact. In fact, you can't touch each other at all, not even to hold hands. You must create sexual tension and anticipation solely through fantasy and provocative dialogue. This exercise will put you in a state of heightened arousal that is reminiscent of the early days of dating before you'd made love.

To recap, here are the steps to creating a Fantasy Encounter:

1. Set aside thirty minutes of quiet time on Sunday.
2. Create your fantasy by mutually developing an erotic story that is arousing to both partners. Be creative.
3. Keep your goals in mind while creating your fantasy.

4. If some parts of the fantasy are objectionable to one partner, eliminate them. Or, adapt them. For example, instead of anal sex, fantasize intercourse in the rear-entry position.

5. Refrain from all physical contact. Stimulate each other through dialogue.

## Elements of the Provocative Encounters

An intense but brief erotic encounter has numerous advantages over a bout of the same old lovemaking—the kind of sex that motivated you to look for a better way. Couples who think sex can't be "good" if it isn't a time-consuming event learn that it can be very good in ten minutes. They expand their definition of *sex* to include mutual masturbation, fellatio, or cunnilingus without intercourse, even intercourse following more mental than physical "foreplay."

The Provocative Encounters are physical encounters that last at least ten minutes and include passionate kissing, manual and oral stimulation of one or both partner's genitals, plus the use of one sex toy. They don't include intercourse during the first week of the program. For couples who've been together a long time, sex without intercourse can seem almost illicit. There's nothing like the feeling of doing something naughty or forbidden to increase desire. Orgasms are, of course, always preferred but not required.

A Provocative Encounter, like the Fantasy Encounter, is a planned event. It may be spontaneous after you've completed the program, but don't wait for the mood to strike now. Planning Encounters creates desire and arousal.

## Here's How It Works

Prepare in advance for the Provocative Encounter by replaying the Fantasy Encounter in your head. Use that scenario as advance mental preparation for lovemaking in stolen moments at work and at home throughout the week, but particularly right before the Provocative Encounter. The Fantasy is mental foreplay.

Select a place and a ten-minute period free of intrusion. Using your Fantasy Encounter to set the tone for the week, agree in advance on what activities will take place during the three Quickies. You may decide to focus on pleasuring each other manually in one Encounter. Another may be designed to give her an orgasm via cunnilingus or him an orgasm via fellatio. Planning is key to the experience because it builds arousal through anticipation.

Incorporate new manual and oral techniques designed to increase arousal and induce orgasm. You must try something new and different in each Encounter. Engaging in a Tantric sex position or stimulating him with a vibrator, for example, may be activities that you've never tried, perhaps because one partner wasn't interested. Remember: You can do anything now, because a Provocative Encounter only lasts ten minutes.

Act as if you feel desire, even if you don't. Couples often discover that a good acting job stimulates real desire. And even if it doesn't, the sexual tension you'll feel afterward will create desire and anticipation for the next Encounter.

Vary your patterns of stimulation in each Provocative Encounter. I tell my clients: Try not to do the same thing twice. Become more daring each week. Maybe your Provocative Encounter will be him bringing her to orgasm manually in the car before going to a dinner party.

When you have intercourse, or a Quickie (Provocative Encounter), use the Fantasy Encounter as mental foreplay frequently throughout the day. A woman may stimulate herself manually before the Encounter to make orgasm more likely. But don't make orgasm an obsessive quest. You can afford to relax. Another Provocative Encounter is only a few days away.

And, don't forget to end all Provocative Encounters with a few minutes of afterplay, the verbal and physical expression of tenderness and affection.

To recap, here are the steps to creating a Provocative Encounter:

1. Prepare in advance. Organize the when, where, and how of Provocative Encounters. And use the Fantasy Encounter as mental foreplay throughout the week.
2. Select a time and space free from intrusions.
3. Incorporate new techniques, new toys, and new positions into the Encounters.
4. Act desire—even if you don't feel it.
5. Vary positions and activities with every Encounter. Don't do the same thing twice! And, don't forget the afterplay.

### The Weekly Evaluations

The weekly evaluation checklist is not lengthy and exhaustive as the questionnaire was. You've already done the in-depth evaluation. The checklist is a quick, easy way of measuring your progress toward goals that week. Most couples find answering these questions less threatening than having to ask or answer the big question, "Was it good for you?"

If you decide together, for example, that the Provocative Encounter didn't heighten arousal for one or both of you, then you will have a better idea of how to develop the next week's fantasy. Were the Quickies not arousing or satisfying? You can examine why they didn't work as well as you'd hoped—and design the next week's encounters with that in mind.

This little weekly quiz takes the personal sting out of evaluating the sex. And, more likely than not, you will find that sex is more exciting and satisfying after the first week alone than it has been in a long time.

## How the Passion Fix Program Immediately Improves Sex

Couples who aren't in the habit of making love anymore need instant results. If they have to wait for a program to work, they'll give up on it. One or the other will say, "This will take too much time," or "We just don't have the time to do it now."

The Passion Fix program works immediately because it:

- *Ends the habit of sexual avoidance.* The "no time for sex" excuse is laid to rest. Couples who have felt disconnected feel as though their connection has been re-established.
- *Gives couples who have been experiencing performance problems the opportunity to "succeed" sexually.* Taking the pressure off a man to get an erection or off a woman to reach orgasm reduces the sexual tension in the

relationship. As long as they are giving each other pleasure and trying something new, they are succeeding.

- *Enhances communication skills.* Couples learn how to listen *and* talk about their fantasies and desires. The questionnaire, goal-setting process, and weekly evaluation quizzes give them a format for discussion of intimate issues.

- *Encourages sexual negotiation.* In working out their sexual differences and control issues to develop a Fantasy Encounter and plan Provocative Encounters, couples learn how to add spice and variety to their lovemaking without feeling coerced.

- *Reduces performance pressure and anxiety.* The ten-minute time frame is not as daunting to a man or woman as open-ended lovemaking.

- *Improves sexual technique.* Couples target their goal areas in Provocative Encounters—and learn new techniques at the same time.

- *Minimizes the problem of disparate desires.* The partners agree to have the Encounters whether they are feeling desire or not. Neither partner has to ask for sex or refuse to have it. More often than not, sexual desire increases throughout the program.

- *Increases intimacy.* Couples feel closer because they are sharing intimate thoughts and feelings as well as having more sex.

- *Heightens arousal.* The process of creating the fantasy and planning and anticipating the Encounters arouses most couples. They typically report experiencing greater arousal beginning with the initial Fantasy Encounter.

## Why Is Sex So Important?

Sex begets more sex. Studies conducted by the National Institutes of Health (NIH) show that the more sex you have, the more you'll want. Why is that good?

*Sex is good for your body.* Lovemaking, particularly if it includes orgasm, boosts production of estrogen and testosterone, improves cardiovascular conditioning, and elevates the level of the brain chemicals associated with desire. But, there's more. Studies have also shown that sex relieves the minor pain of headaches and arthritis and other complaints, possibly because the brain releases endorphins and other neuropeptides, the body's natural painkillers, during orgasm. In women, regular sex can prevent some of the dryness and slackness of muscle tone in the vagina that accompanies menopause.

*Sex is good for your relationship.* Sexual activity helps a couple feel connected to each other. If one partner has been missing sex more than the other, he or she feels more loving now that his or her needs are being met. Emotional and sexual intimacy is enhanced by frequent lovemaking.

## Let's Get Started

No matter how discouraged you and your partner might be about your sex life, you are going to feel better quickly. The 21-Day Passion Fix program gives you the tools for radically improving lovemaking in very little time. It will keep you focused on your sexual goals and give you the ability to meet them easily. Couples who have been unsuccessful with other sexual enhancement programs have been able to make this one work. You can, too.

Now, let's develop your Fantasy Encounter.

PART THREE

# FANTASY
# ENCOUNTERS

## Chapter 4

# Introduction to Fantasy Encounters

## Designing a Fantasy Encounter

If you were sitting in my office, I would help you design a personalized Fantasy Encounter before sending you home to work out the details. We would do that by:

- Going over the questionnaire to determine what you want to improve about your sex life
- Translating your sexual complaints into sexual goals
- Matching your sexual goals with erotic stories designed to set you on the path toward achieving them

I am giving you enough material in Chapters 5, 6, 7, and 8 to help you create Fantasy Encounters. The chapters are organized around similar problem or goal areas (from desire and arousal through orgasms) that lend themselves to the fantasy scenarios suggested. I also give you examples from my practice. I hope the erotic stories of couples who used these fantasies will excite your imagination and get you started.

You will probably want to begin Week One with a Fantasy Encounter that targets your primary goal. Maybe you'll stay with that goal throughout the twenty-one days. More than likely, you'll pick a different goal for each week.

Use these next four chapters in whatever order suits you and your partner.

Many couples need outside inspiration to help them develop their Fantasy Encounters. They might feel awkward and vulnerable sharing their fantasies, especially if those fantasies, as commonly happens, focus on other people. Telling your partner you daydream about sex in a hot tub with his or her best friend probably isn't the best way to kick off a sexual enhancement program. But, who knows? By the end of the twenty-one days, you both might be ready for that.

Some people don't know how to fantasize, because they've never let their minds freely explore erotic possibilities. They censor those thoughts as much as possible. And, some people don't have creative imaginations. They think about sex, but they don't know how to embellish their thoughts to make them arousing to their partner. A Fantasy Encounter is different than a spontaneous fantasy. A fantasy is a solitary and private pleasure frequently stored in the creator's mind and is often not shared with the partner. On the other hand, a Fantasy Encounter is a planned, well-constructed erotic fairy tale in which both partners take responsibility for its creation. This erotic story must be arousing to both partners for it to be successful. To reiterate, in developing a Fantasy Encounter couples are not asked to reveal their personal and private fantasies—this is not the material used in creating a Fantasy Encounter.

I've included a list of suggested books and videos at the end of this chapter. Use them throughout the 21-Day Passion Fix program as resources for Fantasy Encounter scenarios and erotic inspiration before participating in Provocative Encounters. If one partner is highly aroused by material the other finds boring, or even offensive, look for ways to negotiate the difference. What can be added or subtracted from the scenario to excite both partners?

Before you begin reading and watching erotica, take a good look at something more personal, something both familiar and almost forgotten: the beginning of your own relationship. During the initial Fantasy Encounter, I take a couple back to this place and help them rediscover each other. Recall the days when you always had time and energy for sex. What attracted you to each other? What were you thinking about when you couldn't stop thinking about her or him?

Maybe she liked his smile, the dimple in his chin, his broad shoulders, the kindness she read in his eyes. And he liked her shiny hair, sexy legs, pouty lips, sense of style, and the way she handled herself in a spirited disagreement. Her knees went weak when he kissed her neck. He got an erection whenever she made that little move with the tip of her tongue in his ear.

Most couples had a strong mutual attraction to each other when they met. They lavished compliments and attention based on their erotic connection. And then, time passed, responsibilities piled up, and they stopped taking the time to admire each other in words. Tapping into that attraction again while creating a fantasy together stimulates the erotic senses. I instruct couples to use very specific and graphic language to describe their partner's attractive qualities while they're developing a Fantasy Encounter. Find a place for those passionate and tender memories in whatever story you create.

Couples who have done this tell me how exciting and thrilling it was to "rediscover" each other while working out their Fantasy Encounters. "I looked at him through new eyes," a client said. "I focused on him for thirty minutes, recalling the details of our early lovemaking. Suddenly I felt like I had in those days, all fluttery about him."

For some couples, however, there wasn't an intense sexual bond at the beginning. She chose him for his appeal as a provider or rescuer. Maybe he was her "best friend" through a difficult situation. Or he pursued her avidly, and she finally gave in. He picked her over other women he found more sexually exciting because he was impressed by her loyalty and devotion or saw her potential to become the "good wife and mother" he secretly feared a sexier woman might not.

A client once told me, "I met my wife after a woman I loved deeply broke up with me. I thought, *This woman will never break up with me. She worships me.* I was to her what that other woman had been to me. I got married so I would never get dumped again."

If he'd come to me with that story before the wedding, I would have suggested postponing the ceremony, at the least. But he'd been married, more or less happily, for seven years. They had two children together. She wanted more sex. He wanted to find a way to want her. And he needed to find the erotic component of his particular kind of love and desire for his wife.

Beginning with the first Fantasy Encounter, he did.

**The Necessary Components of the Fantasy Encounter**

1.  The thirty-minute time period must be scheduled, not left to happenstance. Anticipation builds sexual tension, too.
2.  Create a space free from intrusion, like the bedroom after the kids are fast asleep.
3.  Be relaxed and comfortable in your clothing and surroundings.
4.  Feign desire even if you don't feel it. Acting can create excitement and stir emotion.
5.  Speak in the present tense and in graphic language, such as "I take your nipple into my mouth and graze it with my teeth."
6.  Create an aura of sexual intensity without touching.

## *Fantasy Encounter Resources*

### *Books*

Allende, Isabelle. *Aphrodite, a Memoir of the Senses.* Harper Collins Publishers, 1998.

Baker, Nicholson. *Vox, a Novel about Phone Sex.* Random House Inc., 1992.

Barbach, Lonnie, ed. *The Erotic Edge: Erotica for Couples.* Dutton/Penguin Books, USA Inc., 1994.

—. *Seductions: Tales of Erotic Persuasion.* Dutton, 2000.

Berkowitz, Bob. *His Secret Life: Male Sexual Fantasies.* Simon and Schuster Inc., 1997.

Britton, Patti. *The Adventures of Her in France* (an erotic adventure novel). Leopard Rising, 2001.

Burton, Sir Richard F., trans. *The Arabian Nights: Tales from a Thousand and One Nights*. The Modern Library, 2001.

Editors of Penthouse Magazine. *Letters to Penthouse Magazine XV*. Warner Books, Inc., 2002.

Friday, Nancy. *Forbidden Flowers*. Pocket Books Inc., 1993.

—. *Men in Love*. Dell, 1992.

—. *My Secret Garden: Women's Sexual Fantasies*. Pocket Books, 1998.

—. *Women on Top: How Real Life Has Changed Women's Sexual Fantasies*. Simon and Schuster Inc., 1991.

Murnighan, Jack, ed. *Full Frontal Fiction: The Best of Nerve.com*. Crown Publishers, 2000.

Nin, Anaïs. *Little Birds and Other Erotica*. Pocket Books Inc., 1990.

Rampling, Anne [Anne Rice]. *Exit to Eden*. William Morrow and Company, Inc., 1988.

Roquelaure, A. N. [Anne Rice]. *The Beauty Trilogy*. Penguin/Putnam Inc., 1985.

Rose, Charlotte. *The Doctor Is In*. Masquerade Books, 1995.

—. *Dangerous Day*. Masquerade Books, 1996.

## Videos

Look for videos produced and/or directed by women for romantic and erotic story lines. Here are a few examples.

Hart, Veronica. *Taken* and *Zazel.*
Royalle, Candida. Anything by her adult film company, Femme Productions.
Shames, Deborah. *The Voyeur* and *Cabin Fever.*

### More Videos and Instructional Erotica Web Sites
Alexander Institute. *www.lovingsex.com*
Dodson, Betty. *www.bettydodson.com*
Grant, Cameron. *The Dinner Party.* A video about different sexual fantasies.
Pacific Media Entertainment (818) 341-3156
Perry, Michael. *www.sexualintimacy.com*
Sinclair Institute. *www.intimacyinstitute.com*

*Chapter 5*

# *Fantasy Encounters to Turn On the Heat*

---

**The Problems:**
- Attraction
- Desire
- Arousal

---

**The Goals:**
- To rediscover attraction
- To create erotic attraction
- To increase desire
- To increase arousal
- To sustain arousal

---

ATTRACTION, DESIRE, AND AROUSAL could be considered the elementary steps to lovemaking. Everyone knows you can have one or two without the other(s) and still have sex. You may not be having sex very often, however, if these three elements aren't in place. Couples who are plagued by lost attraction, low desire, and arousal difficulties often avoid lovemaking because "sex takes too long." What they really mean is that waiting to feel desire or to become sufficiently aroused to have sex takes too long.

Neither partner wants to say to the other, "Honey, I just don't feel desire for you" or "I can't get aroused." Instead, they say, "I'm not in the mood."

## *Attraction*

Rediscovering sexual attraction, or creating an attraction where little existed, sounds like a purely physical activity, but it isn't. Yes, physical appearance counts. Couples who've let themselves go should pull everything back together to some degree with diet, exercise, and a small investment in new clothing and beauty and grooming products. If you've ever seen a makeover segment on a television program, you know what wonders can be worked with a little makeup, the right clothes, and a fresh hairstyle.

But couples can also recreate or build an attraction in their minds by cultivating their garden of erotic memories. One secret to happiness together in old age will be your ability to call up the memories of younger versions of each other. Happy is the man who can hold his wife of forty years in his arms and still see her at twenty standing in the sunlight like a slender goddess with light reflecting off her golden hair. Likewise, the woman who looks back at that man and sees a full head of dark hair and the biceps to match is lucky indeed.

## The Couple

Meg and Paul were facing their fortieth birthdays and didn't want to arrive at that significant juncture with low libidos. Lack of desire was their presenting complaint. Married eighteen years and the parents of two teenage boys, they are lively people who still love each other, but their highly charged erotic memories lay buried under the layers of their hectic schedules. During their initial consultation, each said the other "never seems interested in sex." They also didn't rate themselves as attractive to their mates anymore. But their body language and gentleness with each other made it clear that affection existed in abundant supply.

"I think about initiating sex with Paul far more often than I do it," Meg said. "The idea of making love will occur to me in the morning while I'm driving to work, but by evening so much has gotten in the way of acting out those feelings."

Paul added, "I don't feel right about just grabbing her and saying, 'I want you now.' Shouldn't I wait until there's time to do it right?"

"What first attracted you to each other?" I asked.

The question surprised them, but they had no trouble describing their initial attractions in specific sexual terms. "His green eyes and wide shoulders," Meg said. "She had sensuous lips," Paul said. "And she was wearing a tight red tank top that emphasized her full breasts." Their demeanor began to change as they recalled those first impressions. She laughed, lowered her eyes, and gazed up at him flirtatiously. He reached for her hand.

They were ready to rediscover that immediate, intense physical attraction. Rather than setting their fantasy in the college town where they actually met, I suggested something more exotic. In combining a sensual setting with the memories of their first attraction, they could create a thrilling Fantasy Encounter.

### Their Fantasy Encounter: Sex on the Beach

Meg and Paul re-enacted their meeting on the beach, because both love the ocean but seldom get to spend time around it. In their fantasy, they made love shortly after they met. In real life, they waited until the third date.

Meg, the more sexually inhibited of the two, said she felt "anxious" about making love on a public beach where they might be seen. Paul found the idea of discovery titillating. They agreed that he would arouse her so much she would forget her anxiety. The Encounter, she said, should take place at sunset.

He spotted her standing ankle-deep in the surf watching the big orange sun, as it appeared to sit atop the water on the horizon. Wearing white short-shorts and a blue shirt tied above her midriff, Meg stretched her arms above her head, then put her hands in her hair, and pushed it back off her neck. Paul watched her breasts strain against the fabric of her top, and he got an erection. Suddenly realizing she was being observed, Meg turned to him and smiled. He walked toward her, reached out, and touched a tendril of damp hair that clung to her neck. She put her hand on his bare chest. He kissed her as she'd never been kissed before. Meg let him slip his hand inside her shorts. His caresses had her moaning.

Within minutes they were writhing on the sand. She felt the cold wet sand between her hot thighs and shivered in anticipation of him inside her. With the sound of the waves as background music, they made passionate love. Meg shed her inhibitions along with her clothes and felt no anxiety at all.

## How the Fantasy Encounter Worked

Meg and Paul were surprised at how close to the surface their passionate feelings for each other had actually been—and at how quickly "just talking" could arouse those feelings. Meg also felt less inhibited in real life. Inspired by her fantasy self, she "let down her hair." When he asked her to "dress sexy" for a party that week, she happily complied. "I felt sexy," she said. "I bought a new black dress for the occasion. It was short and fitted, and I knew I looked really hot wearing it."

Both Meg and Paul discovered how "open to suggestion" they were. They were more easily aroused by fantasy than they realized. Yet they hadn't encouraged their own or each other's fantasies until they began the program.

"I look at her sometimes and wonder what kind of passionate thoughts she's thinking and get an erection," Paul said.

## Rediscovering (or Discovering the Hidden) Initial Attraction

1. Was the initial attraction intensely physical? If it was for both of you, go back there. If it wasn't, you'll have to delve deeper into your psyches to find the erotic component of your attraction.

2. Take turns describing how you looked to each other when you met. Remember specific details such as the colors, fit, and style of clothing and how bodies moved

beneath the fabrics. If the attraction wasn't physical, remember details about behavior that impressed you with the strength, intelligence, and ability of your partner. Something attracted you to the other.

3. Express the admiration and desire you felt for your partner then.

4. Recall specific erotic details leading up to the first time you made love. Concentrate on the yearning. Describe how he was aching to feel her hand press against the erection inside his trousers, how she longed to have him caress her breasts and stroke the skin of her inner thighs. Play with the language of details until it's pleasing, and not offensive, to both partners. "Erection inside his trousers," for example, could be expressed in romance novel language as "throbbing manhood." If you didn't feel that intense yearning, retell your story, adding the sexual tension. Pretend it was buried deep inside, and now you've found it.

5. Recall your physical and emotional responses to that first act of love. How did he feel when he finally entered her? How did she feel? Again, add the excitement if it wasn't there.

6. Embellish on that reality to create a fantasy scenario arousing to both of you. Imagine yourselves stranded on a tropical island, living in another time period, or constrained from expressing your love by controlling parents or a cruel spouse in an arranged marriage. Draw on the plots of romantic and adventurous novels and films.

Even couples who think they never had a strong attraction can create that erotic tension and desire if they try. They can find the erotic appeal in those qualities they considered good nonsexual reasons for choosing a partner. He's a good provider? Translate that quality into a fantasy of the dominant man or the rescuing prince who ignites your passion. Cinderella certainly had a passion for that prince. She's a devoted wife and mother? Imagine her as a virgin to be conquered and aroused.

Sometimes the erotic attraction is buried for subconscious reasons. A man or woman may not want to admit feeling an electric tug because that particular kind of attraction feels uncomfortable. Maybe he really wants a woman like his mother, for example, but he has difficulty admitting desire for such a woman *because* she reminds him of his mother. A woman could have similar feelings about the man she married.

## The Couple

Alice, thirty-seven, and David, forty-nine, both busy professionals, had been married four years when they came into my office. "We haven't had sex in two years," he said. Acknowledging that she "never" was in the mood for sex, Alice also claimed that she wasn't sexually attracted to David and, in fact, never had been. He wanted sex. She was thinking about divorce. He was ready to give her a divorce if they couldn't resolve the sexual impasse.

"I don't know if I should stay in this marriage," Alice said, "because sex has become such a big issue for us. If it weren't for the sex problem, I wouldn't want to leave him. He makes my life better in so many ways. I function better with the support of the marriage than I did when I was single. And, I think he does, too. We're a good partnership."

Alice, who projected the image of a strong career woman, was actually dependent on David in a childlike way. That she perceived him as an asexual parent figure became obvious to both of them as they talked about their marriage. Their goal was to sexualize her dependency—to find the erotic element in her attachment to David as the dominant partner. She needed to experience herself as sexual, not childlike, with her husband. But she didn't think that would be possible.

"I've seen other sex therapists," Alice said. "They all told me you can't create sexual attraction if it never existed in the first place."

When I told Alice that she had repressed the sexual component of her desire for David, she wasn't convinced. She also argued that creating a weekly fantasy was too much work. "I don't have the time," she said. But David countered, "It's our last shot at making this marriage work. You can find the time for that." Reluctantly, she agreed to try.

### Their Fantasy Encounter: The Master/Slave

Alice frequently had submissive fantasies in which she was bound by a dominant partner and forced to perform fellatio. She also fantasized being spanked. David didn't find playing the sexually aggressive role attractive. He secretly harbored submissive fantasies of his own, which is not unusual for a man who holds a position of power or authority in his work. As the more nurturing and decisive partner in the relationship, he longed for Alice to take care of him, in general, and sexually, in particular. But as the partner more desirous of having sex, David was willing to make the first concession.

They agreed to fantasize a master/slave scenario in which David held Alice as his sexual captive. But, rather than abusing her, he would tease her sexually, and finally pleasure her, giving her repeated orgasms. The Fantasy Encounter combined her desire to be dominated by him with his interest in the gentler form of domination, teasing sex. An added advantage was that she was available to him in this fantasy as she hadn't been in real life. The idea of having erotic attention focused entirely on her while she was helpless to resist was very exciting to Alice. She started to feel sexual imagining herself in this submissive role. "I love the idea of being totally overpowered and possessed," she said.

In the second week, they agreed to alternate playing slave and master in the Fantasy Encounter, because David wanted an opportunity to be submissive, too. David liked the idea of changing his role. In fantasy, he could make a departure from the responsible role he played in everyday life. Seeing his wife as the sexually aggressive partner made her even more attractive to him. But, alas, there was initial resistance from Alice.

When she understood that he was merely asking her to assume the same authority in her sex life that she did in her corporate life, Alice was more comfortable with the idea. Putting herself in the fantasy helped her become more sexual in real life. Changing the couple dynamics through the use of erotic fantasy is a new concept. It worked for this couple; and it could work for you and your partner, too.

## How the Fantasy Encounter Worked

Alice began to see David in a different, more positive light as soon as they started talking about the first Fantasy Encounter. He became a hero in the kind of romance novels she wouldn't let herself read because they were "frivolous." The submissive fantasy helped her discover the latent sexual attraction she had for her husband. She found his take-charge attitude sexy, although she'd never admitted she did.

Alice was also surprised that she found him attractive in the submissive role. Projecting herself into a dominant sexual role through fantasy allowed her to appreciate the erotic appeal of her own strength. She could also see herself as a woman capable of giving sexual pleasure. For the first time in her life, she felt like an adult.

David was delighted with the change in Alice—and in their sex life.

## Creating a Dominant/Submissive Fantasy

1. The dominant figure in the fantasy isn't a cruel master or mistress. This person gives pleasure. The goal is to excite the submissive partner and prolong arousal before providing release. It's a very powerful fantasy for both partners.

2. The submissive figure receives pleasure. Having pleasure "forced" on them often arouses women who play the submissive. In the scene, they're saying no, but meaning yes. Being submissive relieves a woman, or a man, from the responsibility of becoming aroused. The dominant partner has to do everything.

Sometimes he doesn't want to be responsible for his own erections; and she doesn't want to be responsible for her own orgasms.

3. Light bondage is often part of the scenario. Again, the bonds signify a relinquishing of control and responsibility. The experience is more like going to a spa and turning your body over to attendants who will pamper it, than a hardcore S/M scene.

4. A dominant/submissive fantasy can help a partner with low desire, inhibitions, or sexual guilt issues relax and enjoy sex in the role of the submissive. It can also help a partner who is feeling powerless in the relationship gain confidence in his or her ability to be a powerful lover.

5. Focus on the feelings of desire and arousal created in the submissive partner. Ask him or her to describe these feelings. She might say, "I ache to feel you inside me." He might say, "I feel like I'm going to explode if I don't have you now."

6. Most couples will benefit from switching roles in their later fantasies. Each partner should get to play the one who pleases as well as the one who is pleased.

## *Desire*

Sometimes people confuse *desire* and *arousal*. Desire is the erotic urge that precedes arousal. The two are completely different processes. Many people become aroused and have satisfying sex without feeling desire for each other. Generally, however, when desire remains persistently low in one or both partners, lovemaking declines. Sex can become a vague memory without either partner recalling when or why they stopped making love.

Men and women who suffer from low desire frequently say, "I rarely think about sex anymore." Or, they may say, "Sex isn't on my mind very much." They quickly add their reasons for "not having the time" to think about sex. Everything, from worrying about the crabgrass to monitoring their investments via the Internet, has precedence over sex.

For more than a decade, therapists have designated lack of desire as the "number one sex problem." When the cause of a desire disorder is physical, hormone treatment or other remedies can help. But the reasons for low desire are often more elusive than a low testosterone level or a lack of estrogen. Relationship conflicts, buried anger and hidden resentment, stress, anxiety, depression, side effects of prescription medicines, and many other factors contribute to that "not in the mood" feeling.

Sometimes incompatible desire is really the problem. One partner has a higher sex drive than the other. Maybe they ignored or negotiated around this crucial difference in sex drive in their early years together because it didn't seem like such a big problem at the time. The partner with lower desire was likely more interested both in sex and in accommodating the other than he or she would be as the years rolled by. In the beginning, sex drive is typically high, even for low-desire people. After they've been together awhile, couples settle into their natural desire patterns. Now the higher-desire partner is tired of masturbation as a frequent substitute for lovemaking.

Sexual desire can be rekindled. And, the low-desire partner's temperature can be increased from "warm" to "hot." The change begins in the Fantasy Encounter.

### The Couple

Lorrie and Max, both in their late thirties, were married eight years and had no children when they came into the office. An ambitious couple, each had a frustrating history of disappointments in very demanding careers. Neither had achieved the level of accomplishment and recognition they wanted, but she had been more financially successful than he was. Hard work combined with a lack of real success for one partner takes an especially hard toll on couples. When the higher wage earner is the woman, some couples have problems dealing with their hidden feelings about a woman earning more than her man. He may feel emasculated; she may lose some respect for him.

They came to my office because Lorrie suffered from "depleted sexual desire." She was also, she said, depressed. Initially she claimed that the disparity in their incomes was not a factor in her dissatisfaction with the marriage, but she quickly realized that she'd been kidding herself. It was a problem, for her as well as for him.

"I find Max attractive in general, but I feel no desire for him," Lorrie said. "I'm too tired, stressed, and busy to have time for myself," she complained. "I have nothing left over for him." His "demands for sex" made her angry. "He doesn't appreciate how much of the financial responsibility I carry in this marriage," she said. "He doesn't appreciate me."

Max was equally angry with her—and defensive of his position. "Of course I want more sex," he said. "What's the point of being married if we never have sex?"

Infrequent sex and low desire were their primary complaints, masking other issues. Lorrie was angry with Max because his repeated career problems had forced her to bear the financial burden for the better part of their marriage. "I know he's bright and talented," she said, "but he isn't where we both thought he would be when we got married. When I met him, he was running his own company. He lost it. We've been putting off having children because of his career problems. As his wife, I sympathize with his insecurity, but as the person pulling the load, I want him to get over it and move on."

Although Max felt that he had "let Lorrie down"—and was upset with himself for doing so—he didn't see the connection between that and her loss of desire. They both had to make that connection before they planned a Fantasy Encounter to help them restore the balance of power in their marriage. Problems don't have to be solved before a couple can have good sex, but they do need to be acknowledged. Otherwise, the partners continue to hide behind their excuses for not having sex.

## The Fantasy Encounter: The Ultimate Seduction

As Lorrie and Max were developing ideas for a fantasy encounter, she admitted she once desired him because he was confident, goal-oriented, and authoritative. She saw him as her teacher and mentor as well as her lover. When he was no longer a wise mentor, she lost desire for him. A master/slave scenario, one way of re-establishing a dominant role for Max, was not the best first-choice fantasy for them, although they were able to use it later. Even though she wanted to see Max as a powerful man again, Lorrie had no desire to play the "slave," a role she thought she was already playing in her work life.

Max had to seduce her all over again. In their Fantasy Encounter, he couldn't ravish her at the first meeting the way Paul did Meg in their "Sex on the Beach" fantasy. Lorrie was too resistant to lovemaking in real life for that. He seduced her slowly by plying her with compliments and gifts and paying attention to her. In their fantasy, he took her to an expensive restaurant and listened to her talk about her problems. He put one hand on her thigh; and she felt desire for him coursing through her body. She wanted him to take her in the backseat of the limo that night, but he didn't. He made her wait.

The seduction continued through more long dinners, with his hand moving farther up her leg each time. The Ultimate Seduction leads, of course, to incredible sex, but not until the foreplay, mental and physical, have been prolonged to the boiling point. He didn't make love to her until she "begged" him to take her.

## How the Fantasy Encounter Worked

Lorrie got in touch with the powerful feelings of sexual desire she felt for Max when they first met. Max regained some of his lost confidence just by seeing that his wife could still desire him, despite his career disappointments. He felt more dominant again in the relationship and was motivated to work on his personal career problems.

Planning the Fantasy Encounter also enabled them to talk about the good sexual feelings they shared in the past without eliciting the present anger. Before they began the program, they couldn't have a discussion about sex without the conversation degenerating into accusations and denials. Like many couples, they had lost contact with the sexual part of their relationship. Talking about their nonsexual problems also became easier after they made a sexual reconnection.

## Becoming the Seducer

1. Consider a variation of this fantasy if one partner is more motivated than the other to re-establish the sexual relationship. That partner can play seducer or seductress. Sometimes the more sexual partner can play the reverse role, the one being seduced.

2. The active partner will do most of the talking. He might create a scenario in which the disinterested lover can be pursued but not yet won.

3. Describe the delicious agony of secret desire that she feels while observing the loved one. For example, "I knew he wasn't thinking about me as he lectured the class, but I felt his voice entering the crevices of my body like warm honey. Within minutes, my panties were stuck to my flesh."

4. In graphic detail, explain what he would like to do. For example, "I would tie her to the bedposts with my ties and arouse her slowly with my tongue, licking her body in long, slow strokes until she begged for something more."

5. The passive partner should make suggestions to the fantasy if some elements of it aren't arousing.

## *Arousal*

Sometimes a man or woman desires sex but either can't get aroused or can't sustain arousal during lovemaking with the partner. Obviously a man's arousal problem is more noticeable. He can't get an erection or loses his erection during foreplay or intercourse. His loss of arousal is immediately disappointing, sometimes devastating, to both of them, especially if she can't restore his erection through fellatio or manual stimulation. Both partners consider a flaccid penis during lovemaking an indication of failure.

In a woman the signs of an arousal problem are subtler. Maybe she won't lubricate. Neither her nipples nor her clitoris will become hard. But if she's a good actress, she may be able to convince him that she's "excited" anyway.

The causes of arousal problems vary. Like low desire, insufficient arousal can be the result of physical, emotional, or psychological problems or unresolved relationship issues. Sometimes poor sexual technique is to blame. Women, especially younger women, typically need more time to become aroused than men do. If a man rushes lovemaking, he may be leaving his partner behind.

The bottom line for both men and women is that arousal problems can easily become sexually debilitating. Attraction and desire are supposed to lead to arousal. When they don't, couples get frustrated and start avoiding sex.

### *The Couple*
John, forty-one, and Rachel, thirty-nine, are the parents of

two children, ages six and eight. They came to me because Rachel said she felt little sexual desire for John. As they talked, it became obvious that desire wasn't the problem. Rachel thought about sex and fantasized making love to John. She had desire, but she wasn't becoming aroused when they did make love. So she told him she wasn't "in the mood."

"She never wants to have sex anymore," John said. "She says she loves me, but I'm having trouble believing that. If she loves me, why doesn't she ever want to make love?"

"Sex isn't satisfying for me," Rachel countered. "He takes me for granted. He doesn't spend time on lovemaking. I'm supposed to be ready instantly because he is, but I'm not."

Neither met the other's eyes as they took turns making their accusations. They didn't seem to be connecting on any level. Rachel, who'd been an accomplished professional, decided to stay home with the children while they were young. But she felt inferior in status to her successful husband. John was oblivious to her feelings. He thought she "enjoyed the easy life" at home with the kids. Accustomed to receiving acclaim in the workplace, he had trouble adjusting to Rachel's seeming disinterest in him at home.

"John is emotionally unavailable," she said. "Even when he gets home at a reasonable hour from work, he's on the computer and on the phone for hours. He never stops thinking about work."

Each felt the other was emotionally cold. Both were angry because they felt sexually rejected: Rachel because John didn't take the time to arouse her, John because Rachel kept rejecting his sexual overtures. More significantly, each felt unappreciated by the other.

"We weren't always like this," she said. John agreed. Their sexual situation was all the more frustrating because they'd had a carefree and romantic courtship, one that lasted through the honeymoon and into the early years of marriage. "We would have candlelit dinners at all hours. We turned everything into an occasion. He sent me dozens of daffodils and tulips on the first day of spring. We took horse and buggy rides in Central Park to celebrate the first snowfall every year. We were so romantic!"

Other lovers had also pursued John and Rachel, almost right up to their wedding day. Nothing like competition to heighten the romance! They needed to rediscover their tempestuous romance as a step toward reconnecting sexually. But even before they could do that, John had to make Rachel feel desired and appreciated again. Why did he have to do that before Rachel made him feel desired and appreciated again?

"Is that fair?" he asked. "Yes," I said, because he was the partner more interested in having sex.

If you want sex more than your partner does, you have to put aside words like *fair*.

## The Fantasy Encounter: The Voyeur

John assumed the more aggressive role in developing their first Fantasy Encounter. For them, I suggested an adaptation of a classic voyeur fantasy. John played the man with the telescope observing the unknowing Rachel and becoming increasingly aroused by her as he watched. The Fantasy Encounter took place a week before they actually met. They were neighbors. John found Rachel very attractive, but she hadn't really noticed him at all. He spied on her through his telescope.

One evening as he looked through his telescope, he saw Rachel coming home from work—with another man. He watched them go into the apartment and followed them through the windows as they walked through the apartment into the bedroom. John described how he would feel watching the other man make love to Rachel. As the other man caressed her body, John got an erection. He was in a torment of desire as his rival brought her to tumultuous orgasm with his tongue. "I wanted her so badly, but she belonged to someone else," he said. "I saw her writhing on the bed and longed to be the man who had her there."

When he finally became her lover, he told Rachel how jealous he'd been of this man who'd licked, kissed, caressed, and possessed her. She was excited as much by his jealousy as by the lovemaking. Her orgasm was stronger with him than it had been with the other man.

## How The Fantasy Encounter Worked

The Encounter was titillating for both John and Rachel. She liked imagining herself in the role of a woman desired by two men. For him, the fantasy was thrilling because it set up the theme for the week: John as sexual conqueror. He would take her away from the competition and give her more pleasure than the other man had. Suddenly they both felt validated and desired by the other, something they hadn't felt in a long time.

Rachel didn't think she'd have the energy or the time for romantic/sexual encounters until they shared the first Fantasy Encounter. That changed her mind. They knew it would be hard recreating the magic of their beginning now that the competition was gone and their everyday life was so changed. But once they could finally visualize themselves as romantic, they began to feel "the magic" again.

## Playing the Voyeur

1. Some couples are reluctant to play the voyeur because they consider a person who watches others have sex "perverted." Well, that may be true in real life. But, in fantasy, it is not. Pretend the partner being observed is the star of an erotic film; and the voyeur is merely watching the film.

2. As the voyeur, describe in detail what you see and how it arouses you. Be specific. Say, "I see your rosy nipples glowing against your creamy white skin." And, "As I watch you undress, I feel my body trembling with the desire to touch you."

3. As the object of the voyeur's attention, imagine yourself performing every sensual act slowly. Pretend you are stroking your own body as you undress. As you touch your partner in the fantasy, you can feel the sexual tension multiplied by two because you are being watched.

4. Trade places in later fantasies. Each partner should have a turn playing the avidly desired object of attention and the voyeur.

*Chapter 6*

## Fantasy Encounters to Pull You Out of a Sexual Rut

---

**The Problems:**
- Boredom
- Lack of variety
- Issues surrounding who initiates sex

**The Goals:**
- To alleviate boredom
- To add variety
- To change the sexual pattern
- To balance the erotic power

---

WHILE HABIT AND ROUTINE can be comforting in many areas of life, including lovemaking, they can also lead to boredom and a growing sense of dissatisfaction with sex. Nothing is exactly wrong, but nothing seems altogether right either. What contributes to this sexual malaise? Sociologists and psychologists typically cite factors such as longer life spans (more time together to become bored), social and economic impetus to remain in marriages or monogamous relationships, less time to devote to maintaining a romance, and other equally dispiriting causes. The higher sexual and emotional expectations couples have of their relationships surely play a major role in the "Is that all there is?" lament.

As twenty-first-century couples, we want it all: passion *and* security, romance *and* a full domestic partner, sexual variety *and* monogamy.

Many couples complain of low desire or lament that they have no time or energy for sex because they have let their lovemaking fall into predictable patterns. One partner typically initiates lovemaking, which gives the other partner total veto power, a negative form of erotic power. Or they make love in the same old way every time. Perhaps one partner is reluctant to experiment with new positions or practices—even sex outside the bedroom or making love at any time other than bedtime.

What eventually happens to these couples? Passion cools; desire wanes. One or both lose interest in lovemaking. They are only too eager to believe their own excuses: no time, no energy, too busy, too stressed. Those excuses keep them from looking at what is really wrong: boredom, routine, and predictable patterns that are safe and comfortable. Yet the safe, dull relationship is susceptible to invasion from the outside if the partners don't find that time and energy to make sex exciting again with each other.

When sex becomes routine, some people stray. Others find a way to revitalize and recharge their lovemaking. If you're in a rut, grab hands and climb out of it together.

# Boredom

It's hard to say to your partner: "The sex is boring." Hearing that criticism is almost as devastating to a lover as "You don't do it right" or "You don't turn me on anymore." Most people hear that their partner is bored and take on the responsibility for the sexual malaise. *It's my fault because I'm not sexy enough*, a woman may think. A man assumes: *It's my fault because I'm not a potent lover.* She believes the woman's sexual role is to attract and arouse; he believes the man's role is to perform.

In fact, boring sex isn't one partner's "fault." The gender roles blurred long ago making both arousing desire and practicing good technique the erotic requirements of every lover, male or female. "Boring sex" is a situation a couple creates together; and *they* have to put the excitement back into lovemaking, too.

Each partner can begin to take the boredom out of the bedroom by making nonsexual individual changes as well as changes in their life together. Even a busy, stressed couple can find fifteen minutes each week to go on a walk. What does taking a walk or seeing a foreign film or signing up for dance class have to do with sex?

Almost any positive life change that increases energy is a good beginning for sexual change.

## The Couple

Shelly, twenty-nine, and Adam, thirty-eight, married seven years, are the parents of two small children. When they came to me, they said their sexual problems were all really

Shelly's problems. She had difficulty reaching orgasm, suffered from low desire, and was seldom interested in lovemaking. Adam said, "She's usually too tired for sex. If she isn't too tired, then she says there's no time. I'm frustrated."

Juggling the demands of motherhood and a part-time job, Shelly felt both overworked and underappreciated. "He's more interested in the children than he is in me when he comes home at night," she said. After the preliminary salvos were exchanged, Shelly said something that clearly shocked him: "I don't want to have sex because I'm bored with sex. When I try to make sex more interesting, he won't cooperate."

"Boring?" Adam asked. "You're calling me a boring lover?" He hotly denied that charge. "She doesn't want to try anything new," he said. "If one of us is a boring lover, she is, not me."

In truth, both Adam and Shelly were willing to try "something new," but only if that "something new" was on their own sexual wish list—not on the other's. Adam wanted more "aggressive lovemaking," including anal sex. Shelly wanted to play dress-up. In her fantasy, he admired her in sexy lingerie and made slow, soft, gentle love to her. But in his fantasy, she surrendered to him entirely and had an explosive orgasm via anal sex. Since neither was willing to give into the other, they kept having sex in the same old way. It was a compromise, but a boring one.

"I want an audience," Shelly said. "I want to dress up in lacy black and dance around him until he is aroused. I even suggested going to clubs where we could dance provocatively together while everyone watched, but he said that was perverse."

Adam, who also felt neglected in the relationship, couldn't understand her need to dress up and perform for an audience, especially for other men. He was threatened by her adventuresome attitudes. As the older partner *and* the man, Adam believed he should be the sexually dominant one.

When I suggested they blend their sexual differences into a Fantasy Encounter, they were initially reluctant to try. "How do you blend romance and anal sex?" she asked, drawing a laugh from him. But they finally did come up with a fantasy arousing to both of them—and not "boring" to either one.

### The Fantasy Encounter: The Exhibitionist

I suggested a version of the classic exhibitionist fantasy that allowed Adam to tame his woman after she publicly flaunted her sexuality. In this scenario, Shelly and Adam went to a dance club together on a night away from the kids. She was scantily dressed. All the men in the club turned their heads when she walked in. They couldn't take their eyes off her as she danced provocatively with Adam. Rather than being jealous, Adam was proud that the other men were watching his wife. He knew they were envying him the sex he would have with her later. At one point he licked a drop of sweat from between her breasts. He could almost hear the other men groan.

In the car on the way home, Adam told Shelly sternly that she was a tease. "I'll show you how teases are treated by men," he said. She needed, he thought, a firm hand from a strong man or she would behave more and more outrageously. There was a limit to how far he would let her go in tempting other men. In their bedroom, Adam ripped the flimsy dress from her body. Shelly stood before him in a G-string, garter belt, stockings, and very high heels. They were both panting.

Slowly she began dancing for him, gyrating her hips and thrusting her pelvis so close to his crotch that he felt his penis straining to break through his trousers to claim her.

When he couldn't stand the excitement any longer, Adam grabbed her. They made love hard and fast, with him entering her from behind. They came together in an explosive, noisy orgasm. Afterward he slowly and gently brought Shelly to multiple orgasms using his mouth and his hand.

### How the Fantasy Encounter Worked

The fantasy was more arousing to both of them than either thought possible. Adam shed his feelings of insecurity when he projected himself as the one man in the room capable of taming this sexy exhibitionist. Shelly enjoyed the idea of being taken aggressively—after she'd been allowed to flaunt her charms. Both found the more gentle lovemaking at the end of the fantasy a stirring epilogue to the main event.

Developing their Fantasy Encounter also enabled Adam and Shelly to mesh their differences in lovemaking through the Provocative Encounters. He acknowledged that he still had misgivings about his wife dancing suggestively in public. But she was content to put on a private show for him at home—and pretend she had a wider audience.

---

### Merging Sex Styles

1. If your fantasies and secret desires don't easily mesh, you need to be imaginative in devising a scenario that contains elements pleasing to each of you and not offensive to either. It's okay to propose and discard

several ideas before settling on the one that arouses you both. But you need to be equal contributors.

2. Keep an open mind. Close your eyes and imagine being inside the fantasy your partner suggests. Maybe you can fit there after all.

3. Rather than throwing out a concept one partner likes—for example, bondage—find a way to adapt it. If she is reluctant to be bound, she may suggest, "My wrists are not tied to the bed, but I put my arms over my head and grasp the bed railing tightly."

4. Include some familiar erotic practices, such as deep kissing or gentle caressing, at the beginning and end of the story.

## Variety

Some men, and women too, believe that sexual variety is only possible with more than one partner. They claim that monogamous sex may not be boring if the partners are creative lovers, but it can't offer variety. Only changing partners can do that.

They're wrong, of course. You can create sexual variety by adopting different sexual practices with the same partner. Too many couples think that sex equals intercourse in one of the two basic positions. Sex can be mutual masturbation or one partner pleasuring another manually or orally. It can include toys, costumes, and props, or it can incorporate ancient Eastern lovemaking techniques. If sex is always a few minutes of foreplay followed by intercourse, it's lacking in variety, whether you have more than one regular partner for the routine or not.

There are also times in life when intercourse either isn't possible or satisfactory. During the late stages of pregnancy, for example, mutual masturbation or oral sex is frequently preferable to intercourse. Medical conditions, sometimes associated with age, can also make intercourse difficult for men with erectile difficulties. But they can still have "sex."

### The Couple

Sharon, fifty-three and Larry, sixty-one, the parents of two teenage children, had been married eighteen years when they came into the office. Larry had recently completed treatment for prostate cancer. The treatment had left him impotent (although this occurs in a minority of prostate cancer patients), but doctors assured him that he could still enjoy a sexual relationship with his wife. Larry, however, was afraid to try.

"We stopped having sex altogether while he was ill, and I tried to understand," Sharon said. "But I miss lovemaking. I'm tired of waiting. I don't even feel sexy or desirable anymore."

Sharon felt she'd been a "supportive wife" and couldn't understand why, for the past two years since being diagnosed with cancer, Larry had been sexually and emotionally unavailable. She didn't realize that he felt old and sexually inadequate. "I'm afraid I'll never be able to please her again," Larry said. "That part of my life seems to be over."

Sharon didn't think sex was dependent on an erect penis, but Larry did. She loved the creative ways he would touch and pleasure her "in the old days, before he became so obsessed by his penis." He argued, "Cunnilingus is fine in addition to

107

intercourse, but how can I feel like a real man if that's all I can do?"

They needed a fantasy that would restore Sharon's sense of herself as desirable *and* expand Larry's definition of how a real man makes love. I suggested that Larry begin developing a powerful fantasy about Sharon, one that would not make him feel pressured to perform. As he thought about the fantasy, he realized he'd always wanted to ask her to masturbate for him but never had.

### The Fantasy Encounter: The Eunuch Lover

Sharon wanted to develop a fantasy based on a sexual encounter that took place when they were dating, before they'd had intercourse. Larry had aroused her and brought her to orgasm with his hand inside her panties. She could still recall the way he had caressed her face, breasts, and thighs before stroking her clitoris. But he remembered his own erection throbbing while he pleasured her; and he wanted a fantasy completely removed from that past reality.

They settled on a fantasy in which she was an Egyptian princess and he was one of the eunuchs who served her. He worshiped her, but she hardly noticed him. He watched her undress for her bath and longed to touch her full, ripe breasts and the round curves of her belly. Her skin was luminous and velvety. She seemed mesmerized by her own body, oblivious to his silent presence as he waited to serve her. One day she began masturbating, bringing herself to orgasm, while he watched in the shadows.

At her moment of ecstasy, she looked into the eyes of her eunuch, seeing him for the first time as he trembled, barely able to control his desire to worship her body with his hands and mouth. She smiled. "Maybe someday I will let you do this for me," she teased him. He lived for the moment when that might happen. While he waited for her summons, he consulted a high priestess on how to please a woman; and she taught him secret techniques for his tongue and his fingers. At last the day came when the princess called him to her chamber. "Please me," she commanded. He brought her to orgasm over and over again using his fingers and tongue to stimulate her genitals in ways she had never imagined. "You are the best lover I've ever had," she told him when she was finally able to speak.

## How the Fantasy Encounter Worked

Sharon took the lead in developing the fantasy, but Larry quickly jumped in. Adding the masturbation element helped equalize their situation because he felt as though he, too, was making a request of her for something she found embarrassing in real life. He was surprised to discover he got aroused just talking about the fantasy.

Afterward Larry told her that he'd never believed her when she said, "Lovemaking isn't just about intercourse." He thought that she'd been trying to protect his feelings. Now he, too, had an expanded definition of sex. Both saw this fantasy as an opportunity to be more creative in their lovemaking. Larry realized that his ability to please and be pleased sexually wasn't compromised by the failure of his penis to achieve erection.

Sharon said she had never felt more desirable. The Fantasy Encounter helped them begin to restore their sexual chemistry. It also boosted their individual sexual self-confidence levels.

## Creating a Sex Goddess

1. If one partner, most often the woman, has a poor body image, the other partner should take the lead in creating a sex goddess (or god) fantasy.
2. The sex goddess (or god) is the object of tremendous desire. Her body parts are described as erotic glories.
3. The aroused partner describes his (or her) responses to the slow unveiling of the beautiful body in very specific terms. "As she lowered her gown over round ivory shoulders, I began to sweat. My breath caught in my throat in anticipation of the joys to come as the cloth slipped farther down her silken skin." (If those words are initially too embarrassing to speak or hear, begin with the more flowery and less specific language often found in many romance novels.)
4. The goddess (or god) can intensify the story line by letting her admirer know that she secretly desires him even as she casts a cool glance at him.
5. At first, the goddess (or god) should be observed either in the bath, stroking her own skin, or in the act of masturbation, even being intimate with another man.
6. Their sexual union is postponed until the worshiper is out of his (or her) mind with desire.

## *Initiating Sex*

A generation ago, the man most often initiated sex. Numerous surveys and research studies show that the pattern of initiation has changed over the years. Men still are more likely to suggest sex than women, but the gap is closing. In some relationships, initiating sex is a fifty-fifty proposition.

When one partner, man or woman, initiates sex most of the time, that person would seem to hold the erotic power in the relationship. But that's not necessarily true. The partner who frequently says no may hold the real power card. Both can easily get stuck in their roles of initiator and rejector with a predictable result: less sex.

Breaking a rigid pattern of sexual initiation in a relationship is good for both partners. The one who was always asking for sex will feel more desired when he or she is the one invited to play. And the partner who passively waited for an invitation can enjoy being the aggressor or seducer for a change. *Remember:* You can't climb out of that rut if you aren't willing to make a change.

### *The Couple*

Jeff and Cindy, both in their late thirties and the parents of a ten-year-old son, were the couple friends described as "perfect." A freelance designer and avid amateur photographer, he managed their home and family life while she traveled frequently on business. They insisted that her higher income and important job title didn't give her more power in the relationship. But in one significant way it did. She was the partner who most often didn't have time for sex. He was more easily available, a position that can dampen desire in both women and men.

"I wouldn't say I initiated sex more often," Jeff said. "It was more like begging or nagging for sex. I quit doing that. Now I can see for myself she has no time, there's no point in asking."

"If he asked more often, I'd make more time," Cindy said, but she admitted that her hectic travel schedule, especially in the past year, had made "asking" more difficult.

Keeping passion alive when one partner travels frequently or routinely puts in long days at the office is difficult for a couple with a great sex life. A couple trapped in rigid sex roles is unlikely to succeed in sustaining passion under these circumstances. I helped Jeff and Cindy develop a Fantasy Encounter that they could use as a model for phone sex when she travels. He took the lead in outlining a scenario in which she was entirely at his erotic disposal. For once, he didn't have to ask. She was eager.

### The Fantasy Encounter: The Film Director

Jeff played the role of a famous film director while Cindy was an actress struggling for recognition. He cast her in a highly erotic film being shot on location outdoors in Istanbul. She was eager to please him, on camera and off, but he didn't seem interested in her. He made her shoot take after take of a demanding scene. She played a captured spy forced by a cruel despot to dance, slowly strip, then caress her breasts, and stroke her vaginal lips. The script called for her costar to humiliate her verbally in front of his men before taking her off to his bed and raping her. By the time Jeff was finished with her, she had captured the part of an exhausted hostage perfectly.

Jeff realized that she was weak, heavy with the desire to be possessed and used solely for a man's pleasure. He had enslaved her. After dismissing the cast and crew for the day, he led her by the hand back to his trailer. "Get down on your knees," he ordered her. "And satisfy me." She sank to her knees, hungrily took his penis into her mouth, and complied.

### How the Fantasy Encounter Worked

To her astonishment, Cindy loved the submissive role Jeff created for her. At home she embellished the story with her own responses. Eagerly she described how she would feel as a young actress completely under the command of one of the cinema's greatest directors: "I loved having a break from being responsible, dependable, in control. Pretending I had no power made me feel free. It was an incredibly sexual feeling for me."

Jeff found his role very arousing. The fantasy helped him see himself as a powerful man, capable of making a strong woman weak with desire for him. Instead of asking or begging for sex with his wife, he said, he would be less diffident in the future. "Once in a while, a man has to say, 'I want you, woman! Get in here!'" he said.

---

### Restoring the Balance of Erotic Power

1.  This is a role-reversal fantasy. The partner who seems to control the relationship based on a higher income and especially less time for sex allows the other to play the dominant role. Or the dominant partner may be

the one who controls the sex, either by always initiating or by usually refusing.

2. The fantasy should contain elements of control the partners can accept; for example, being seduced by someone who has great influence over his or her professional life. And, the submissive partner should be in a situation where his or her time is completely at the other's disposal.

3. Each should describe in detail the erotic feelings associated with this power exchange. A woman playing the submissive role may say, for example, "Waiting for you to notice me, touch me, I felt myself melting, my insides melting, turning into a molten core of desire. I craved your hands, your mouth, your penis."

## Chapter 7
# Fantasy Encounters to Intensify Sex

---

**The Problems:**
- Performance anxiety
- Performance difficulties
- Poor erotic technique
- Difficulty reaching orgasm

---

**The Goals:**
- To reduce performance anxiety and improve performance
- To improve technique
- To increase frequency of orgasm
- To increase orgasmic potential

---

HOW IMPORTANT are good technique and the ability to perform sexually?

A man or a woman can be an adequate lover, maybe even a good *enough* lover, with modest technical skills. He or she can never be a great lover without a diverse bag of sexual tricks. Great lovers are passionate and romantic—the qualities praised by those who disparage skill—but they have the skills, too. Inexperience and poor lovemaking skills can douse the fires of passion.

On the other hand, a man, and sometimes a woman, can worry so much about performance that he or she become anxious. Performance anxiety may or may not hinder lovemaking ability, but it certainly diminishes the experience for the anxious partner. He or she watches and silently criticizes his or her performance rather than actively participating in lovemaking. This process of mental withdrawal is called "spectatoring," because it turns a lover into a spectator at a sexual event, not an involved participant in the lovemaking.

Performance problems, performance anxiety, and a lack of lovemaking skills all take their toll on an intimate relationship. Couples like this often complain of low desire or lack of time and energy for sex. Avoiding lovemaking becomes easier for them than dealing with disappointment and frustration when the sex doesn't "work" the way they fantasize that it could and should.

And fantasy is the first step toward making that good sex life a reality, not a wish or a dream.

## *Performance Anxiety*

Male performance anxiety is rooted in the erection. If a man can't get an erection as soon as he begins to feel aroused, he worries. If he loses his erection during lovemaking, he feels embarrassed and worries about what his partner will think and how he will be able to please her if he can't stay hard. Concern about getting an erection and maintaining it for a suitable length of time during intercourse can distract him from love-making.

Instead of ignoring his penis and pleasing his partner in other ways, he turns the focus on himself. Often they both work at trying to restore the flagging erection when they should leave it alone and turn their attention to arousing and satisfying her. Ironically, her arousal is more likely to get him excited and erect again than anything else they could do specifically "for" him.

Women have performance anxiety, too. As one client who agonized over her fellatio skills said, "It isn't just about having thin thighs anymore. Women have to know what to do, too." Like men, they worry that they aren't "good" in bed. Some women avoid performing fellatio because they fear their technique is inadequate. Others feel uncomfortable in certain intercourse positions, especially female superior, because they don't think they perform well in those positions.

Both women and men sometimes avoid trying a new position or practice because they fear "doing it wrong" and looking foolish. Self-conscious behavior inhibits lovemaking. Couples who have lived with performance anxiety in one or both partners are delighted to discover how much fun sex can be when they get past those insecurities.

### The Couple

"I never had this problem before," Peter said. Anxiety probably led to his erectile difficulties with his live-in girlfriend, Angela. Both in their early thirties, they had been living together almost two years when they came into the office. "I try hard to please Angela," he said. "I've never wanted to please a woman as much as I do her because I love her."

Peter's anxiety over pleasing Angela was exacerbated by her own evolving sexual behavior. She wanted him to be a more aggressive lover. In the early days of their relationship, she didn't share her fantasies with him. After they'd been together more than a year, Angela felt comfortable asking him to act out a bondage scenario, playing master to her slave. Peter experienced the requests of his more sexually experienced girlfriend as threatening demands. "I'm a gentle, caring lover," he said. "I don't see myself like that."

"I don't understand what's going on with Peter," she said. "He was a good lover. Now he loses his erection during intercourse or he comes too quickly. I feel like he's blaming me because I asked for something I wanted. And that makes me mad!"

Clearly this relationship wouldn't last if Peter couldn't accept and participate in Angela's fantasies—as well as find a cure for his chronic erection problems.

## The Fantasy Encounter: Erotic Bondage

Angela was immediately enthusiastic about developing a fantasy encounter, but Peter felt uncomfortable and awkward. As she talked, however, he became aroused by her bondage fantasy and began to make suggestions for improving it. In their fantasy, he played a master lover rather than a "master." He tied Angela to the bed with silken scarves to drive her wild with ecstasy, not to prove his total control over her.

Angela was a driven businesswoman who never had time

for the kind of lovemaking he longed to have with her. Tired of their hurried encounters, he followed her to London on business and took a room next to hers. She was stunned when he knocked on her hotel room door, took her into his arms, and said, "I am going to take you somewhere you've never been before."

Lovingly he kissed and caressed her while slowly removing her clothes. When she was naked, she begged him, "Take me now." Instead he blindfolded her, tied her to the bed, and skillfully brought her to orgasm after orgasm with his fingers and tongue. Finally he removed the blindfold, entered her, and brought her to one last shuddering climax.

## How the Fantasy Encounter Worked

Peter discovered the hidden power in Angela's fantasy: It made him feel like her equal as a lover. The fantasy both aroused him for the Provocative Encounters that followed and made him more confident of his ability to be successful in them. Projecting himself into the role of a sophisticated and superior lover reduced his performance anxiety for the first time in months.

He became so focused on being more aggressive sexually that eventually he was distracted from his performance anxiety. As a result, his erection and rapid ejaculation difficulties disappeared. Peter said, "I didn't realize how excited Angela would become in the passive role. That helped me see her in an entirely new way."

Angela was delighted with "the new, improved Peter." She said, "I feel like he has finally and totally accepted me and embraced my erotic side. I love him better this way."

## Fantasizing Restraint

1. Bondage fantasies can be elaborate tales woven around intricate bindings or as simple as an aggressive lover holding together the wrists of his partner during love-making. Restraint is the key. The restrained partner is held down by the partner who hasn't felt equal in the sexual relationship.

2. As in a fantasy of dominance and submission, the bound partner is pleasured. She (or he) may be held captive or forced to receive pleasure and may even struggle against it. In this game, the bound partner doesn't submit.

3. The aggressive partner performs as a superior lover, melting the resistance of his (or her) partner with erotic skill.

4. The bound partner should describe how she (or he) feels in restraints. She may say, "I am angry that you're holding me; and I'm trying to resist your power. But your hands and mouth are setting my body on fire."

5. The aggressive partner should describe what he is going to do to his captive. He may say, "I am going to lick and suck you until you beg me to mount you . . . but I won't. Not yet."

## *Technique*

Many couples avoid lovemaking that has grown routine and boring because they simply never developed their erotic skills. They may have entered marriage with little sexual experience or many unacknowledged inhibitions. Maybe she fell into the habit of faking orgasms and then didn't know how to tell him he wasn't pleasing her when she grew tired of faking. One or both partners might have praised the other's performance of oral sex or another form of lovemaking while privately feeling disappointment. They don't want to criticize, so they say, "Great sex." But sex isn't like a dinner party hosted by friends when a polite response to a bland dinner is a social requirement.

Difficulty in asking for the kind of stimulation they need to become highly aroused and reach orgasm also prevents many men and women from giving their partners the kind of guidance everyone needs to become a good lover. They're sending silent messages: *Stroke my clitoris. Kiss me deeper. Suck my nipples.* And they can't understand why their partners aren't getting those erotic directions they're too shy to speak out loud. Embarrassment and inhibitions create a bedroom climate in which good technique isn't likely to flourish. A couple has to be willing to share erotic information and practice new skills together before they become proficient.

If one partner, particularly the man, comes into the relationship with considerably less sexual experience, both may find talking about technique particularly difficult. He thinks he should "know" what to do in bed. Maybe she thinks he should, too.

Suggesting "let's both learn something new" can prevent a discussion about technique from turning into a lecture on how one partner could improve in bed.

## The Couple

On their first visit to my office, Sophie, thirty-nine, literally pulled her boyfriend Frank, thirty-seven, by the hand. During the two years they'd been together, she'd consistently had difficulty becoming aroused during lovemaking. Sophie was "beyond frustrated" with their sex life and angrily blamed Frank for their problems. "He doesn't know how to please me," she said. "I've told him what I like, but he doesn't do it. He isn't even a good kisser. Because I'm never sufficiently aroused to lubricate, intercourse is often painful. But he doesn't care as long as he gets his pleasure!"

Sophie read his failure to please her sexually as a form of rejection. On the other hand, Frank, who was an inexperienced lover, felt tremendous anxiety over his failure to arouse Sophie whom he very much loved and desired. "She's demanding and critical," Frank said. "There is just no pleasing Sophie. She says she tells me what she wants, but she's never really that clear about it."

Sophie and Frank were in a sexual stalemate. Each felt hurt and rejected by the other. Sophie was right when she said they wouldn't stay together if they didn't resolve their sexual issues, but she was wrong to place all the blame on Frank.

## The Fantasy Encounter:
## The Sexual Genie in the Bottle

Both Sophie and Frank initially resisted the genie fantasy because it was "silly." Neither one knew how to be playful in bed. When they got into the game, however, they discovered they liked it. In their fantasy, Sophie was shipwrecked on a deserted island. Among the lush flowers and fruit, she discovered a beautiful bottle, its stopper inlaid with precious stones. While rubbing the sand off the belly of the bottle, she felt it shake. The stopper blew off. Amid a swirl of smoke, a genie appeared. And he said, "I can grant your every sexual wish. But you must tell me what you want in exquisite detail."

Sophie lay back in a bed of flower petals and asked the genie to perform oral sex. She told him to begin by kissing her, from her mouth to her breasts, and then down her body. "Lick the insides of my thighs with long, slow strokes of your tongue until I feel giddy with desire," she told him. He did as she instructed. When she was ready, she told him exactly how to lick and suck and kiss her vagina and clitoris. He brought her to such orgasmic heights that she passed out in a delirium of pleasure.

### How the Fantasy Encounter Worked

Sophie found this fantasy to be an exciting way of asking for what she wanted sexually. "Pretending" gave her an excuse to become playful about sex. She relaxed and stopped behaving as if Frank were a pupil who must be continually instructed, monitored, and corrected. "The fantasy lifted us out of our same old problems," she said.

Frank saw the fantasy as an opportunity for learning better

techniques. He used books and videos as resources. And he found this a "less threatening" way to learn about how Sophie wanted sex. "Sophie wasn't interfering," he said. "Everything was up to the genie. He was responsible for pleasing her, but she couldn't tell him how to do it. Fantasizing her in this role was liberating for me."

Sophie finally felt that Frank was really trying to be the lover she needed him to be. Through fantasy, Frank was able to identify with the sexual genie and eventually see himself succeeding in that role.

---

## How to Become the Perfect Lover

1. Sometimes one partner is much more skilled than the other. But in most couples, both partners need to improve their technique. Take turns developing the fantasy so each partner has a chance to play the one who pleases and the one who is pleased. The speaker directs his or her partner and then accepts direction.

2. Describe how you want your partner to perform in careful detail. Say, "Now run your tongue slowly up and down the shaft of my penis." Or "Take my breast in your hand and squeeze it softly."

3. Focus on how these actions will make you feel. For example, say, "When your tongue moves in long, slow strokes alongside my clitoris, my whole body stands at attention and quivers in anticipation."

4. Add to the fantasy by having the genie express his or her feelings about how arousing that role is. He might say, "In all the centuries I've been jumping out of the

bottle and pleasing women, you are the woman who has excited me the most. Your skin has the texture of orchid petals. You taste like a honey liqueur."

## The Second Couple

Sam, thirty-three, and Nina, twenty-eight, a newlywed couple, came to see me because he was experiencing difficulty maintaining an erection during intercourse. As they talked about "his" problem, it became clear that Sam wasn't getting the kind of stimulation from Nina that he wanted. "With previous partners," he acknowledged, "I became very aroused by fellatio. Nina isn't comfortable performing fellatio. She gives me a few licks and that's it. I need more."

"I don't mind performing fellatio," Nina said defensively. "I just don't think I'm very good at it. I gag if I take his penis too deeply into my mouth. And if I suck on him a little bit and he doesn't get hard right away, I'm disappointed. But, if he is really hard, I stop because I don't want him to come in my mouth."

Although Frank assured her he wouldn't let that happen, she didn't quite trust him. They needed a fantasy that would put Nina in the erotic driver's seat while satisfying Sam's desire to get the oral stimulation he craved. This time the genie had to be the woman.

## The Fantasy Encounter: The Genie in the Bottle

Sam had an inventive take on the classic fantasy. He purchased a book on "how to be a better lover," thinking he'd bought something that would tell him how to please Nina.

But the book was written for women on pleasing men. Disappointed, he fell asleep on the sofa, the open book on his chest. Suddenly he was jolted awake. The book moved. A genie who looked a lot like Nina appeared before him.

"I am here to pleasure you," she said, falling to her knees. "Tell me what you want."

Sam gave her graphic instructions on how to perform fellatio. She followed his directions perfectly. When he could stand no more, he signaled to her that he wanted to ejaculate. She removed her mouth and brought him to climax with her hand.

**How the Fantasy Encounter Worked**

Nina loved the sense of erotic power this fantasy gave her over Sam. She was capable of driving him wild with fellatio— and still controlling the encounter to the point where she "finished him" manually. That image helped her see fellatio as a skill to improve lovemaking rather than a service to be performed.

Sam was highly aroused by the fantasy. In this scenario Nina gave him what he most desired, and she loved doing it. Their sexual communication was also greatly enhanced.

And the idea of the book inspired both of them. They went to a bookstore and purchased several sex guides. "We would have been too embarrassed to buy those books in the past," she said.

## *Orgasms*

Previous generations of women claimed that it was "the closeness" and "the intimacy" of lovemaking they craved—and orgasms didn't matter. Either they were lying or they didn't know what they were missing. Orgasms do matter, for both men and women. Yes, it is possible to enjoy lovemaking occasionally without orgasm. But if lovemaking seldom, rarely, or never leads to orgasm—the sexual frequency rate will precipitously decline.

Even more common than female anorgasmia—or the inability to reach orgasm—is this complaint: Orgasm takes too long. That is one of the most common reasons women give for saying no to sex. When achieving orgasm is a marathon event for a woman, she may fall into the habit of avoiding sex unless they have time for a long, leisurely lovemaking session. And how often can most busy couples arrange that?

Increasing a woman's orgasmic potential and improving the quality of the orgasmic experience for both partners will almost guarantee that they'll have sex more often.

### The Couple

Laura, fifty-two, was reluctant to get involved in sex therapy. Gary, her husband of four years, insisted they get help. Laura had never experienced an orgasm alone or with a partner. "I enjoy sex anyway," she said. "It doesn't matter. Gary wants me to have an orgasm because it will make him feel better. His ego is on the line. He thinks he should be able to give me an orgasm, and he's frustrated that he can't."

"We are having sex less and less often," Gary countered, "because orgasm is an issue. I don't believe she's fine without one. And I am frustrated because I can't give her the ultimate pleasure. Is that male ego? I want her to feel good. I don't see what's selfish about that."

Laura argued that their careers were so demanding there was no time for sex therapy. Orgasms were a luxury she couldn't afford. Gary insisted orgasms were a necessity they couldn't live without.

## The Fantasy Encounter: Playing Doctor

Laura became visibly anxious at the mention of a fantasy encounter. She claimed she never had sexual thoughts or fantasies during lovemaking or at any other time. "When we make love, I don't think about the details of sex. I am filled with love," she said.

She said she couldn't talk about sex; let alone create a Fantasy Encounter with her husband. Surprisingly, Gary wasn't enthusiastic about the idea either. Both argued against the "prescriptive nature" of the Fantasy Encounter. "Sex should be more natural and spontaneous," Gary argued. Other important events happened in their lives because they planned them, I said. Why not plan sex? And, how much natural and spontaneous sex were they having now? They finally consented to try.

Laura and Gary enjoyed going to the movies together. In fact, when Laura was younger, she considered an acting career. I suggested she play an actress in a medical drama. Following an automobile accident, she is paralyzed. But doctors have been unable to discover why she has no feeling from the waist down. Gary plays a specialist flown in from New York City to examine her.

When he walked into the hospital room, her heart stood still. He was the handsome prince of her dreams. As he spoke gently to her and began examining her, she thrilled to his touch. To her surprise, she had feeling below the waist. As he held her leg in his hand, caressing her calf, she moaned slightly. "Am I hurting you?" he asked. "No," she whispered. "It feels good."

He massaged her calves and thighs. His hands kept moving, exploring her body between her legs. She had never felt such intense sensations as he explored her vagina. He held her clitoris gently between two fingers. Writhing in delicious agony, she begged him not to stop. And he gave her an orgasm, the first of her life.

## How the Fantasy Encounter Worked

Laura began to experience herself as a sexual person. She could imagine letting go and allowing Gary to take care of her erotic needs. Neither of them realized how sexually creative she could be until they developed this fantasy together.

"The doctor fantasy stayed in my mind," Laura said. "I thought about it at work and other places."

Gary said, "The fantasy also removed the pressure to give her an orgasm. Once I could imagine it happening, I believed it would someday and didn't feel stressed about when."

The Fantasy Encounter was very arousing for both of them and also restored Gary's sense of power in the sexual relationship.

## Playing Doctor

1. This fantasy celebrates one partner's erotic discovery of the other's body. The roles don't have to be doctor

and patient. One partner could be feigning sleep as the other strokes, caresses, and kisses his or her body.

2.  The partner playing patient or sleeper experiences his or her body being sexually awakened inch by inch. Describe how that will feel. She may say, "Your hand caressing my ankle sends tiny electric shivers up my leg and into my vagina." Or, he may say, "You run your nails lightly inside my thigh; and my penis becomes erect."

3.  Take turns playing the roles. Each partner should enjoy this wonderful sensual experience as each part of the body comes erotically alive under a lover's touch.

*Chapter 8*

# *Fantasy Encounters to Enhance Intimacy*

---

**The Problems:**
- Poor communication skills, especially sexual communication
- Lack of closeness in the relationship
- General sense of not feeling connected to each other

---

**The Goals:**
- To improve sexual communication
- To elicit a dialogue about the sexual relationship
- To enhance intimacy
- To restore feelings of closeness and affection toward each other

---

WOMEN ARE MORE LIKELY than men to complain about the lack of intimacy in a relationship, but men also experience feelings of loss when this primary emotional bond is weakened or strained. Although they may have been taught to express their needs and desires in different ways, both men and women want to feel connected to their partners. Men typically think that closeness is maintained through frequent love-making, while women believe conversations about feelings sustain intimacy.

When a couple has little time for each other, the love-making *and* the intimate conversations are postponed. Because they aren't having as much sex as they want or the kind of sex they would like to have, they may not find lovemaking as emotionally satisfying as it once was. Again, they blame time constraints or their depleted energy levels.

What really contributes to the intimacy drain? All the factors we've previously discussed, including problems with desire, arousal, performance, and technique can play a role in creating a wedge between partners because they contribute to a decline in the frequency and quality of lovemaking. Communication—that overworked modern buzzword!—is also an issue. Couples who can't talk to each other about their sexual needs, desires, and dissatisfactions aren't likely to have a highly satisfying sex life.

Partners who have "no time to talk" probably have "no time for sex" either.


## Communication

Everyone from members of talk show audiences to friends giving advice can expound on the importance of "communication" in a relationship. But communication has two parts: talking and listening. Too many people focus on the talking aspect. They just don't listen, especially if they don't want to hear what's being said.

Women frequently lament that "he never talks to me about his feelings." Sometimes that complaint really means: "He isn't telling me exactly what I want to hear about what he's feeling." An empathetic listener can hear the emotional component of a lover's words and accept the other's "feelings," no matter what they are. His feelings won't always conform to her idea of what those feelings should be.

Sexual communication, in particular, requires skill. Partners need to say "I want" rather than "You don't give to me . . . " or "You don't . . . " Speaking in descriptive language also helps get the sexual points across. "Touch me" isn't much help. But when you add exactly how and where and for how long you want to be touched, you've made an erotic request as arousing as it is hard to refuse.

Communication is sometimes nonverbal as well. Sighing, moaning, gently moving your partner's hands or mouth to where you want them to be, or shifting positions during intercourse are all forms of nonverbal communication that get your message across and help your partner please you. *Thank you!* scribbled on a note stuck to the mirror on the morning after great sex can be more meaningful than a sonnet.

### The Couple

Ron, fifty-six, and his wife, Ilene, fifty-two, had just celebrated their twentieth wedding anniversary when they came to see me. They would soon have an empty nest, with both sons in college. Ron said, "I'm bored with our sex life. I know we're missing out on what should be great years for us. She never expresses sexual pleasure, either through words or moans, when we make love. Maybe I never have really pleased her. If that's the case, I have to wonder what we're doing together. Why don't we split up and look for happiness before it's too late?"

Ilene indignantly insisted, "I enjoy our sexual relationship!" The problem, she insisted, was that he wanted her to be someone she wasn't. "I'm not noisy in bed. That's just not my style. I can't believe he doesn't know if he pleases me or not. He's bored, and he's looking for an excuse to blame me. Ron is always dissatisfied. That's his attitude toward life in general."

But he would not let her dismiss his complaints or requests by saying, "Oh, that's just Ron!" He was very clear about what he wanted from her as a sex partner. "I want her to initiate sex more often and participate more actively when we do make love. I want her to tell me what she likes, what she wants, how I make her feel."

Ilene protested that she felt "awkward" talking about sex, especially "when we're doing it." She added, "I don't think a woman has to moan and carry on like a porn star to show sexual pleasure."

Finally she acknowledged that changes would have to be made in their sex life to make Ron happy. He seized on the concept of the Fantasy Encounter as a good beginning for adding "more variety and spice" to their lovemaking. Reluctantly Ilene said, "I'll try."

## The Fantasy Encounter: An Erotic Fairy Tale

Ilene simply could not create a Fantasy Encounter with Ron. "I love him and I want very much to please him, but I can't," she said. She couldn't transcend her embarrassment and overcome her inhibitions, so designing the fantasy became Ron's complete responsibility. Ilene agreed to participate if he would write the script.

Ron devised an erotic fairy tale in which the beloved queen, Ilene, finally lost her sexual inhibitions and learned how to express her love for the king in the most graphic and carnal ways. If the queen didn't do that, Ron said, she would lose the king to a spell cast by an evil witch. The spell could only be broken by Ilene's cries of ecstasy.

Try as she might, the queen could not produce a groan of pleasure in her long lovely throat no matter how ardently the king made love to her. Desperate, he brought a bag of sexual toys—such as handcuffs, lotions, feathers, and even a vibrator—into their royal bedchamber. The queen's face began to show unmistakable signs of pleasure as he oiled and massaged, kissed and caressed, stroked and pleasured her with his body and each device at his disposal. He longed to hear her explode in one low guttural howl as his fingers expertly stroked the slick, tender skin around the sides of her firm, pink clitoris. But, no matter how hard he tried, the sounds would not pour out of her mouth.

Exhausted, the king fell into a troubled sleep. The moonlight shone over their bed as he tossed and turned, haunted by the specter of the witch and her spell. The queen watched him sleep. She kissed each grimace in his brow. When a tear escaped the corner of his eye, she kissed that, too. She sighed. Then she sobbed.

Stroking his penis until it became erect, she whispered declarations of love to her sleeping king. When he was hard, she mounted him. She rode him, slowly at first, then faster and faster until he awoke. Leaning forward on her braced arms, she kissed his lips. Drops of sweat fell off her forehead onto his. Her body shook and shivered. As she came, she cried out loudly and repeated the cry over and over again. She had saved the king.

## How The Fantasy Encounter Worked

Ilene laughed at the fantasy, pronouncing it "silly" when she read the script. But she was able to participate, in spite of feeling "awkward," because she convinced herself she was playing a dramatic role. Soon she discovered she liked the role. She saw the queen as a woman whose great emotional depth was both matched and contained by her great sense of dignity. She was, after all, the queen. Ilene could relate to that woman because it put her silence in a different, kinder perspective.

Each week they used the same Fantasy Encounter with additional embellishments. By the third week, Ilene was improvising and adding sexual directions for Ron. "I did find the fantasy arousing," Ilene admitted.

Both Ron and Ilene said the fantasy helped them talk about sex in a nonblaming, nonthreatening way. They rediscovered an emotional intimacy they hadn't experienced in years. Ron knew how difficult it was for Ilene to put herself into the fantasy the first time, and he was touched and gratified by her efforts.

"I feel closer to her because she was willing and able to do this for me," he said.

### Creating an Erotic Fairy Tale

1. The mutual storytelling technique typically works best when both partners create the story together. This cooperative effort is particularly effective at opening up lines of communication between partners who just don't talk anymore.
2. Begin the story with "Once upon a time . . . " because that phrase automatically leads us to think in fairy-tale terms.
3. Pick a setting, occupation, or historical period that has always seemed interesting or romantic to at least one partner.
4. Take turns embellishing the story line. Develop the scenery. Linger over the fine points—for example, the purple, green, and gray colors of the sky as the monsoon blew into Bombay.
5. Strew obstacles in the lovers' path, prolonging the sexual tension before the inevitable sweet release. (Read a romance novel to see how that's done.)

## Intimacy

Some couples believe that "intimacy" can only be achieved and maintained by working hard on the relationship. Other couples develop a deep intimate connection that doesn't seem to require a lot of maintenance. Their different approaches to nourishing the relationship are likely rooted in their own personalities. Some people, particularly men, have trouble letting their guard down completely, even with a life partner. For them, "opening up" isn't natural and may require some effort. I often tell women who complain that their husbands aren't good at intimacy to "make love more often." After lovemaking, men are more apt to share their feelings than at any other time.

Women, on the other hand, tend to downplay the role of good, hot sex in creating and sustaining intimacy. Sex isn't the extra "something nice" in a relationship some women like to think it is. Sex is the glue that holds partners together.

When a couple hasn't made love for a while, they begin getting on each other's nerves. The rough edges of the relationship are standing up, ready to scratch them. Sex smoothes those edges.

### The Couple

Brad, thirty, and Cynthia, twenty-eight, had only been married a year when they came into the office. Cynthia suffered from very low sexual desire and had difficulty reaching orgasm. Brad was both frustrated and puzzled by Cynthia's lack of interest in sex because their lovemaking had been passionate and satisfying before the wedding. She blamed her sexual malaise on Brad, whom she labeled "emotionally distant."

"Since we've been married, Brad has been putting in long hours at the office and frequently traveling," she said. "He comes in late, maybe after being out of town for two days, and wants to jump me. I can't work up the enthusiasm for instant sex with someone who barely has time to say hello."

Brad suggested, "Maybe we should go on dates again. I was working hard when we were dating, but she understood. She was eager to see me when I got back from a few days on the road."

But Cynthia said, "Getting our sex life back on track isn't going to be that easy. I have a more demanding job now than I did last year. We have two hectic schedules to work around, not just one."

As they talked, Cynthia and Brad realized that she was lonely in the marriage. "I thought we would be so close," she said wistfully, "and we're not."

### The Fantasy Encounter: Rediscovering First Love

Brad and Cynthia had a romantic beginning. They met in Paris where each was traveling with friends. In creating a Fantasy Encounter about their initial attraction, Cynthia wanted to regain the immediate emotional chemistry they shared as well as the physical chemistry. "We communicated through body language," she said. "I felt as though I knew him before we had a real conversation."

I suggested a fantasy that would recreate the emotional intensity Cynthia craved. Brad suggested revisiting their meeting exactly, but Cynthia wanted a scenario more removed from reality. She quickly invented a young woman who had recently moved to France. "She doesn't speak French and she's lonely, very isolated. It's been a long time since she had a lover and she's longing for a man. Sometimes at night she tosses and turns until the sheets are twisted between her hot legs."

Brad wanted to create the male character. "There is a Frenchman," he said. "He doesn't speak English. He is a regular in the café on the corner of the Rue St. Jacques where she lives in a tiny attic apartment. He sits alone at an outdoor table watching her walk past and undressing her in his mind."

Cynthia said, "One night she sees him watching her. She looks into his eyes, and she knows exactly what he's thinking. That night she pretends he is in her bed. She closes her eyes and feels his mouth covering her nipple as she slides one hand between her legs."

At home, Cynthia and Brad developed the fantasy into story about a couple who communicate via sex alone and fall deeply in love before they ever have a real conversation. The urgency in their desire and need for each other is over-whelming. They must overcome many obstacles to be together for one night of incredible passion. And that night is so wonderful they vow never to part.

## How the Fantasy Encounter Worked

Developing this story together had a powerful effect on Cynthia and Brad. "We became lovers again," Cynthia said on the second visit. "We were excited about each other."

The Fantasy Encounter aroused them and also revealed the true source of Cynthia's sexual problems. She needed to feel deeply loved and desired by Brad again. Once the emotional bond was restored, Cynthia's sexual interest and ability to orgasm returned.

That might not have happened without sex. "I didn't understand why she was withholding," Brad said, "but I knew she was. The more she withheld sex from me, the more I pulled away from her. Having her show an interest in being my sexual partner again made a big difference to me."

## Taking a Fantasy Trip

1. Almost any fantasy can be changed, and maybe improved, by setting the story in an exotic locale. Choose a place that seems romantic to you both, whether you've been there or not. Then do a little reading—perusing some travel guides will do—to give your story some local color.

2. Leave your inhibitions behind, along with your daily routine. You have no responsibilities or strong attachments to anyone, except your lover. All your senses are heightened. You are free to indulge them.

3. Linger on the physical details of your meeting and the seduction. Say, "Under the bright sun of Cairo, you, with your blonde hair and blue eyes, are a rare and lovely vision."

4. Or pretend there is a language barrier. You can only communicate through gestures—and lovemaking.

5. To heighten the sexual tension, pretend you are star-crossed lovers, an Arab sheik and a Western journalist, for example.

*Chapter 9*

## Evaluating the Fantasy Encounter

## The First Fantasy Encounter Report Card

Every one of the couples you've met in these four chapters successfully used the Fantasy Encounter to create sexual tension and set the erotic tone for the week ahead. Why are these encounters so effective?

- The couples created them. The stories represent their own fantasies and desires. A therapist did not superimpose them. When it comes to erotic fantasy as an arousal tool, one size does not fit all.
- Beginning with a fantasy encourages creativity in later behavior. Sex really does begin in the brain, the very area where modern couples have shut the process down. They think they can shove sex to the back of their minds all day and have their bodies magically respond at night, but they can't.

- Describing the fantasy helped the couples visualize new ways of making love.
- By expressing feelings through storytelling, the couples shed some of the inhibitions that have kept them from asking for what they want sexually. It's easier to be bold in a "pretend" situation than in "real life."
- Learning about new sex techniques became easier through the fantasy venue.
- The couples began to see each other in a new way through fantasy, which opened up possibilities they hadn't considered in real-life sex.

## *Fine-Tuning the Fantasy Encounter*

How effective was your initial Fantasy Encounter? Answer the following questions together to rate your own progress. If the Fantasy Encounter wasn't as effective at creating desire and arousal, you've still learned something.

1. Did the fantasy contain elements that were arousing to each partner?
2. Were you able to negotiate the details—for example, changing bondage to holding her hands together over her head, or making love in a public place to making love in your own hot tub after midnight?
3. Did you share in creating the fantasy and embellishing the details?
4. Was the story familiar enough to be comfortable but different enough to be exciting?

5. Did the Fantasy Encounter set the tone for the Provocative Encounters to follow?
6. Did you find yourselves thinking about, perhaps even discussing, the Provocative Fantasy hours or days afterward?
7. Are you feeling sexier? Are you viewing your partner as more sexually appealing?

# PART FOUR

# PROVOCATIVE ENCOUNTERS

## Chapter 10

## *Introduction to the Provocative Encounter*

The Provocative Encounter will

- Change the way you define sex
- Reignite that sexual attraction
- Increase desire in both partners
- Intensify arousal in both partners
- Improve lovemaking skills
- Increase the intimate, romantic connection between partners
- Help each partner overcome sexual problems
- Make lovemaking more creative, more interesting, and more satisfying on every level

I promise that you will never dismiss the "Quickie" as an inferior substitute for the real thing again! Before couples begin the 21-Day Passion Fix program, they define *sex* as intercourse. The majority of modern couples define *foreplay,* as some kissing, caressing, mutual manual genital stimulation, and at least the "lick and a promise" version of oral sex—

cunnilingus for her, fellatio for him. No wonder these couples aren't having "sex" very often anymore. They don't always have time for their routine of foreplay that briefly touches all the bases leading up to intercourse culminating, they hope, in orgasm for both of them. If you throw in the romance requirement—some candles, a glass of wine, dinner together to create "the mood"—the average couple probably has time for "sex" once a week, if they're lucky.

"Lovemaking has to last long enough for her to reach orgasm during intercourse," male clients often say in explaining why they seldom make love. Other couples may avoid "sex" because they're having problems with his erection or her orgasm. Making love for a prolonged period only accentuates their problems. And some couples are "too tired" or "bored" or "just not in the mood." They certainly aren't inspired to find the time for lovemaking. For all these couples, "sex," as they have defined it, isn't very satisfactory anymore.

When they redefine *sex,* they open the door to erotic possibility. They become playful again. If you don't think that's possible, give the 21-Day Passion Fix program a chance to work magic in your life. Imagine what you and your partner can do together if you take your sex life out of a confining box. Sex can be an imaginative adventure, not a chore or an obligation.

The Provocative Encounter pulls a couple out of the typical sex-equals-intercourse lovemaking routine, with a refreshing new focus on pleasure. Although the Encounters are planned events, the sex becomes more unpredictable and more thrilling because it breaks the stale pattern. In fact, during the first week of the program, I ask clients to abstain from intercourse altogether. Their Encounters can include passionate kissing, oral sex, manual stimulation, mutual masturbation, one partner bringing the other to orgasm fully clothed—but no intercourse. Why?

*Not* having intercourse heightens the sexual tension. By the second week, most couples are desperately eager for intercourse. Couples who have performance anxiety or technical problems really benefit from delaying intercourse. With the pressure to perform removed, they can relax and enjoy giving and receiving pleasure. For any couple in a monogamous, long-term relationship, sex without intercourse seems almost illicit, like the beginning of an affair. Many clients tell me that the first week of the program made them feel as if they were just starting to date again.

In Chapters 5 through 8, you saw how couples with different sexual issues and problems used their Fantasy Encounters as mental foreplay to increase desire and arousal in anticipation of the Provocative Encounters ahead. The next set of chapters, 11 through 14, follows those same couples in their Provocative Encounters. I'll explain why they chose the Encounters they did as well as describe how the Encounters worked for them. I hope you will be able to relate to the examples and use them as ideas in developing your own Provocative Encounters. You'll find plenty of additional help for doing just that in the following pages.

Because we can all learn a new skill or improve an old one, the Provocative Encounters chapters also feature tip boxes with easy to follow step-by-step advice on everything from kissing techniques to intercourse positions. I've included these tips because I want you to have everything you need to become a great lover in twenty-one days. But you don't have to try everything in three weeks! Some techniques may not appeal to you or your partner now. Maybe they will later. Consider this book a reference guide, like a cookbook you can use again.

If you have any lingering doubts about the effectiveness of Quickies, put those doubts aside—and get ready to plan a Provocative Encounter. By the end of the first week, you and your partner will be more erotically charged and sexually satisfied than you've been in a long time. You'll also find that daily problems seem somehow more manageable. Smoothing the rough, abrasive edges of being coupled is the bonus of good sex.

Couples who aren't satisfied with their sex lives probably aren't feeling emotionally close to each other either. They're apt to be fighting about other issues as well. Because they don't have a good sexual relationship, they don't have an easy path back to each other through that forest of harsh words and resentful feelings. They need to develop or renew a passionate connection *quickly* before they can resolve conflicts, sexual or otherwise.

The Provocative Encounter does all that—and more.

## The Necessary Components of the Provocative Encounter

Now let's talk about the basic components of the Provocative Encounter. You must plan and schedule three, and each should last for at least ten minutes. Remember that variety is the spice of life, and of sex. So, without further ado, the following list explains how to do it.

1. *Planning.* Schedule the three encounters and don't let anything—short of a medical emergency—interfere with the plan. Select a time and place free of intrusion. Have the first encounter early in the week, on Monday or Tuesday.

2. *Timing.* Each encounter should last at least ten minutes. That time period is important. First, even the busiest couple has ten minutes. Second, the brevity of the experience makes it seem less daunting for a couple who may have performance anxiety or other issues.

3. *Tapping into the Fantasy Encounter.* Get ready for a Provocative Encounter in your head. In stolen moments the day of the scheduled event, draw on your Fantasy Encounter for advance mental stimulation. This is your mental foreplay—your "no hands" arousal secret.

4. *Stimulating genitals.* Every Provocative Encounter includes both manual and oral stimulation to one or both partner's genitals. During the first week, intercourse is not allowed. In the second week, sex toys are added. And, by the third week, all Encounters should include an intercourse Quickie and the use of a sex toy.

5. *Varying the stimulation.* Vary patterns of oral and manual stimulation from week to week. Use the sex toys more creatively each time. Try a different variation of a Quickie intercourse position each time. Don't do the same thing twice! Be more daring and creative each week.

6. *Orgasms.* Orgasms are preferred but not required. Making orgasm an obsessive goal may take the fun out of the Provocative Encounters. On the other hand,

you may be surprised and perhaps relieved to discover that you both can have an orgasm in ten minutes.

7. *Afterplay*. Spend a few minutes cuddling after the Encounter. Compliment each other. Afterplay often opens the door for intimate communication and sharing feelings.

## *Provocative Encounter Resources*

### *Books*

The following books are divided into categories. The first group is made up of general sex guides.

Bechtel, Stephan and Laurence Roy Stains. *Sex: A Man's Guide*. Rodale Press Inc., 1997.

Block, Joel. *Secrets of Better Sex*. Parker Publishing Company, 1996.

—. *Sex over 50*. Parker Publishing Company, 1999.

Rosenthal, Saul. *Sex over 40*. P. Teacher Inc., 1987.

The next group of books focuses on detailed sex advice— some of it rooted in Eastern lovemaking techniques—for couples who want directions for advanced sex.

Annand, Margot. *The Art of Sexual Ecstasy*. Tarcher/Putnam Inc., 1988.

Bakos, Susan Crain. *Sexational Secrets*. St. Martins Press, 1996.

—. *Still Sexy: How the Boomers Are Doing It*. St. Martins Press, 2000.

—. *What Men Really Want*. St. Martins Press, 1990.

Cox, Tracey. *Hot Sex*. Bantam Books, 1999.

Keesling, Barbara. *Sexual Pleasure*. Hunter House, 1993.

—. *Super Sexual Orgasms*. Harper Collins Publishers, 1997.

Kuriansky, Judy. *The Complete Idiot's Guide to Tantric Sex*. Alpha Books, 2002.

Paget, Lou. *How to Be a Great Lover*. Broadway Books, 1999.

—. *How to Give Her Absolute Pleasure*. Broadway Books, 2000.

*The Big O: How to Have Them, Give Them, and Keep Them Coming*. Broadway Books, 2001.

Finally, the last group of books addresses sexual dysfunctions, with a strong emphasis on solving problems.

Berman, Jennifer and Laura Berman. *For Women Only: A Revolutionary Guide to Overcoming Sexual Dysfunction and Reclaiming Your Sex Life*. Henry Holt and Company, LLC., 1999.

Foley, Sallie, Salley Kope, and Dennis Sugrue. *Sex Matters for Women: A Complete Guide to Taking Care of Your Sexual Self*. Guilford Press, 2001.

Ladas, A.K., B. Whipple, and J.D. Perry. *The G Spot: and Other Recent Discoveries about Human Sexuality*. Holt, Rinehart, and Winston, 1982.

Leiblum, Sandra and Judith Sachs. *Getting the Sex You Want: A Woman's Guide to Becoming Proud, Passionate, and Pleased in Bed*. Crown Publishing, 2002.

Zilbergeld, Bernie. *The New Male Sexuality*. Bantam Books, 1999.

## Videos

In the past few years, there has been an explosion of educational sex videos. The following are some of the best.

Dodson, Betty. *Celebrating Orgasm* and *Sex for One.*

Pacific Media Entertainment (818) 341-3156. *The Complete Guide to Sex Toys and Devices, The Lover's Guide To Sexual Ecstasy,* and other videos in the Sexual Enhancement series.

The Sinclair Institute (*www.intimacyinstitute.com*). *Becoming Orgasmic, Sexual Positions for Couples, Complete Guide to Sexual Positions, You Can Last Longer,* and other videos in the better sex video series.

## Where to Purchase Materials

Here are some places to purchase educational materials, videos, books, and sex toys.

Adam & Eve Catalogue

(800) 765-ADAM, *www.adameve.com*

Their bestselling products include Dr. Ruth's Eroscillator, a smaller, streamlined, quiet vibrator with detachable heads for different kinds of stimulation. The company also coproduces and markets high-quality erotic films and instructional material.

Patti Britton, Ph.D., sex coach

*www.yoursexcoach.com*

Dr. Britton features her picks for videos, sex toys, and more on her entertaining and educational Web site. She also answers questions about all aspects of male and female sexuality.

Good Vibrations
(800) BUY-VIBE, *www.goodvibes.com*
The grandmother of sex toy shops, Good Vibrations has a retail store in San Francisco and runs Cleis Press, which publishes *The New Good Vibrations Guide to Sex: Tips and Techniques from America's Favorite Sex Store,* by Cathy Winks and Anne Semans.

The Xandria Catalogue
(800) 242-2823, *www.xandria.com*
Their catalogue is an interesting mix of the tasteful and the tacky. In addition to the usual products, books, and videos, they also market excellent publications on such topics as sexuality and cancer, and on sexuality and disability. These booklets contain information on where to buy specialized products to aid sexual expression, other resource information, and fine illustrations on adapting sexual positions and skills to the situations.

*Chapter 11*

## *Provocative Encounters*
## *to Turn On the Heat*

---

**The Problems:**

- Attraction
- Desire
- Arousal

---

**The Goals:**

- To rediscover attraction
- To create erotic attraction
- To increase desire
- To increase arousal
- To sustain arousal

---

EACH OF THE COUPLES you met in Chapter 5 had a primary sexual goal derived from their problems with attraction, desire, and arousal. Their Fantasy Encounters were designed to spark or revive attraction, increase desire, or heighten and sustain arousal. Each couple accomplished the goal but naturally had varying degrees of success in doing so. Remember that every couple starts out in a different place.

If your Fantasy Encounter didn't help you and your partner meet your goal in the first week, at least to some mutually agreed-on extent, you need to revise the script and try the new, improved scenario in week two. The weekly Fantasy Encounter is the foundation for the three Provocative Encounters. You tap into that mental erotic energy as foreplay to arouse you for the Quickie event. If the fantasy doesn't excite both of you, try another one. Lukewarm mental foreplay just isn't hot enough.

The four couples were at different levels of desire and arousal as they began the first week of Provocative Encounters. And that's fine! When you read their stories, you may identify with one couple more than the others, probably because they seem to be in the same stage of erotic readiness both before and after the Provocative Encounter as you and your partner are. Feel free to borrow elements of their Fantasy Encounters when you design your own.

By the end of week one, each of these four couples reported feeling more sensual, more attractive to and attracted by their partners, and more aroused before and during love-making. They also felt a renewed emotional and intimate connection to their spouses. After investing one hour total in their sex lives for one week, they had all achieved progress toward their sexual goals that they wouldn't have believed possible before they started the 21-Day Passion Fix program.

This new and positive sexual attitude carried over into other areas of their lives, too. For example, they began paying more attention to personal grooming and to wearing more attractive clothing around the house. Some husbands agreed to save their most offensive (to their wives) "comfortable" old clothes for doing outdoor work, not lounging on the sofa. All four couples said they felt more energetic, more alive, and more optimistic about their ability to resolve conflicts and negotiate differences together.

Sex has healing powers that can seem almost magical sometimes.

## *Attraction*

When men and women begin to feel more attractive to, and attracted by, their partners, they almost always have more interest in making love. Feeling attractive is as important to an intimate relationship as feeling recognized and valued is to a working relationship. "I don't feel sexy" often means, "I don't feel attractive to my partner."

### *The Couple*

Meg and Paul used their initial Fantasy Encounter, "Sex on the Beach" (page 82) to help them rediscover the strong and immediate attraction they had for each other the day they met. When they came into the office, they both had low desire. After eighteen years of marriage, they had relegated "sex" to the back burner of their life together. Both said, "My partner doesn't find me attractive." They were, however, affectionate and gentle with each other—and had no difficulty summoning memories of those early days when their mutual sexual attraction was intense. Their Fantasy Encounter gave them an opportunity to revisit the erotic past and stage their introductory meeting under more romantic circumstances, against the backdrop of sand and sea.

"That Fantasy gave us a sexual jump-start," Paul said. "We both wanted to go back to the beginning and feel the way we'd felt then. We were so playful with each other. And we'd lost that quality altogether in later years."

Meg added, "We really needed to feel like newlyweds again. I can remember when my hands trembled when he came close to me. The Fantasy helped us go back and experience the electric charge again."

Their Fantasy Encounter was enormously successful in bringing their dormant erotic feelings back to life. Meg and Paul were surprised at how quickly "just talking" aroused both of them. They designed their first Provocative Encounter as an erotic massage with Paul playing the masseur irresistibly drawn to his client. In the second Encounter, they took advantage of their heightened state of arousal generated by the Fantasy and the massage in a "make-out session" that was reminiscent of their real first date.


### *The Provocative Encounter: The Make-Out Session*

"We made out on our first date," Meg said. "I was so aroused by the kissing and caressing that I really wanted him, but I was determined not to go all the way on a first date."

They scheduled their second Provocative Encounter for early Wednesday evening when their sons were at soccer practice. "And it wasn't our turn to carpool," Paul said, laughing wryly. For ten minutes, they made out on the sofa in the family room, recreating their first make-out session.

"Before we lay down together, we took off our tops just like we did that first night," Paul says. "But the bottoms stayed on. I'll never forget how excited I was to see and touch Meg's breasts. They were so beautiful; and they still are."

Entwined in each other's arms, they described their feelings for each other the first time they kissed and touched. She told him how much she loved his chest hair and the fullness of his biceps. He told her she was the most beautiful woman he'd ever seen—and that her lips had been driving him crazy with lust since he first saw them.

"I shivered when he touched my breast," Meg said. They caressed and stroked each other, their fingers expressing their remembered wonder and delight. And they kissed—the way they hadn't kissed in years.

"He took a long time kissing me, first kissing each lip, then pulling back to lick my lips with the tip of his tongue, before kissing me again. I'd forgotten how much that little kissing move of his turned me on. By the time he French-kissed me, I was weak with excitement."

They finished the Encounter by caressing each other's genitals through their clothing and rubbing against each other. They both reached orgasm, almost simultaneously. "That was an unexpected event for both of us," Meg said. "It was thrilling and made us long for intercourse."

"And it was better than our first date," Paul added, "because we had orgasms."

## How the Provocative Encounter Worked

Like their Fantasy Encounter, this Provocative Encounter

was very successful in achieving their goals. In ten minutes on the family-room sofa, Meg and Paul were transported back in time. They experienced the intense chemistry and the almost unbearable sexual tension of their first date.

"We both felt we'd met our week's goal of rediscovering erotic attraction and increasing desire with the Fantasy Encounter and first Provocative Encounter, the sensual massage," Paul said. "Achieving the goal so easily made us realize that our sexual potential was greater than we'd realized. We were capable of having an exciting sex life, but we'd settled for quiet and boring."

The Make-Out Session is an ideal Provocative Encounter for a couple who are trying to revive a sexual attraction that was intense when they were younger. But occasional make-out sessions can make any couple feel young again. Making love like this, including simulated intercourse, is sometimes called "outercourse," because some clothing remains on, or "noncoital sex," signifying no penetration. (Readers of a certain age may remember when high school kids called it "dry humping.") Some couples only practice noncoital sex in the last stages of pregnancy or following surgery or injury. But they're missing something by not playing like teenagers in love more often.

Making out and stopping short of "going all the way" feeds sexual tension and creates desire for intercourse. If you thought only couples in new relationships could long to have intercourse together, you're wrong. Deny yourself the pleasure—and see how hungry you can become.

**Technique: The Perfect Kiss**

- Brush your lips lightly across your partner's lips. Pull back. Take his face in your hands. Put your lips on his and press gently as you look into his eyes.
- Explore her lips one at a time with light, playful, teasing kisses.
- Close your eyes and kiss him passionately—without inserting your tongue.
- Kiss her lightly again. Now, French-kiss. Remember to use the tip of your tongue to play with your partner's tongue, inside of lips, edges of teeth. Don't thrust your tongue forcefully into her mouth.

## *The Couple*

Alice and David had to discover their sexual attraction, not rediscover it. Unlike Meg and Paul, they didn't have wonderful sexy memories of their first date. When they came into the office, they'd celebrated their fourth anniversary and hadn't had sex in two years. David was frustrated to the point of threatening divorce. Alice said she'd "never" been attracted to him and had married him because she felt safe with him. "I love him," Alice said, "but I don't lust for him." David was an asexual parent figure to her. How could they build a sexual attraction from that?

While Alice had misgivings about the idea, she and David developed a "Master/Slave" theme (page 86) for their Fantasy

Encounter. That Fantasy helped her begin to see David in a different, more sexual way. She was finally able to tap into the erotic component of her attraction for him and realize he was more than her "daddy" after all.

Alice and David developed the first week's Provocative Encounters on the Master/Slave theme. Neither of them wanted to act out scenarios of dominance and submission that included spanking or other "serious" practices. (Most couples use the Master/Slave game as a metaphor for the exchange of erotic power, not as a real exercise in discipline. The game also gives them a structure with assigned roles for giving and receiving sexual pleasure.) David, as the "master," focused erotic attention on Alice, "forcing" her to become excited. Her bondage role allowed her to relax her inhibitions, let go of responsibility for feeling desire or arousal, and be pleasured by her husband. David was the strong seducer she could not resist; and Alice was the helpless "victim" of lust.

## The Provocative Encounter: Tie and Tease

David tied Alice to the bedpost with fur-lined feminine handcuffs. He used an ostrich feather in long, sweeping strokes on her breasts, inner thighs, and genitals to arouse her. Next David applied warm scented oil to her body and gave her an erotic massage. He brought her to orgasm with a vibrator. David and Alice used sex toys in their first week of the program, although they aren't required until the second, because they had used them in the past. In their second and third Provocative Encounters that week, David stimulated Alice with different sex toys, stroked her with velvet gloves, and, covered her body with rose petals before massaging her.

"Alice wasn't ready for oral stimulation in the first week," he said. "We saved that for the second week."

By the third week, Alice consented to playing the mistress to David's bound slave. She cuffed him to the bed and pleasured him both manually and orally. Both were comfortable with sex toys—and used them in creative ways. For example, Alice strapped a small vibrator to the back of her hand while she gave David manual genital stimulation. It was, he reported, "a mind-blowing sensation."

## How the Provocative Encounter Worked

David felt more desirable and attractive to Alice in the first Provocative Encounter. But not until the third Encounter did she say "something nice" was beginning to happen for her. They both were actually pleased to see progress that early in the program.

"I never thought my wife would feel sexual desire for me," David said. "I was pleased and flattered that she was feeling something by the end of the first week. That was a lot more than I'd expected."

Alice said, "I was amazed to feel a sexual attraction to David. That changed the way I felt about him. I also enjoyed being the focus of his attention in a sexual way. I wasn't being a helpless girl with him for a change."

Both Alice and David were "cautiously optimistic" about achieving their primary goal, creating sexual attraction for David in Alice, by the end of week one. Their ability to be "playful" with each other following the Encounters was an unexpected benefit for both. That sex could be "fun" was a revelation for Alice.

"Tie and Tease" is a good Provocative Encounter for any couple. It is particularly successful when one partner, such as Alice, is less desirous of sex or more inhibited than the other. The master or mistress who controls the pleasure gets an ego boost while the slave is relieved of all sexual responsibility, including arousal. No one feels pressured. In that atmosphere, desire and arousal will likely develop.

### Technique: Tie and Tease

- Assume a comfortable position. The best position for most people is sitting up with the back against the headboard, arms to the sides, and wrists fastened to the bedposts.
- Use gentle restraints, such as Velcro handcuffs or loosely tied silk scarves or ties. Do not use metal handcuffs or tight knots. The "slave" should be able to work his or her hands loose if desired.
- Tease with your mouth and hands, applying only as much pressure as will arouse your partner. (Don't, for example, tickle to the discomfort point. Instead, use a feather and softly run it up and down your partner's body.)
- Vary the pattern of teasing strokes, from passionate kisses to gentle caresses.
- Use fabrics, feathers, flower petals, oils, lotions, and other sensual materials.
- Focus on the pleasure points: nipples, on both men and women; inner thighs; backs of knees; the neck; ears; the line from the navel down to the pubis; and

the genitals, including the perineum in men. (The perineum is located between the base of the scrotum and the anus.)

## Desire

Sexual desire can be elusive. It's hard to summon on demand, even when partners still find each other attractive. Sometimes the more a woman or man wants to desire a partner, the less they do. Again, stress and tension play a role. You feel as though you should want sex. Then you feel guilty because you don't, even though you "try."

Desire has to be coaxed gently, not demanded. It has to build from the inside out.

### The Couple

Lorrie and Max came to see me because she felt no desire for sex. Max was angry with her for continually refusing his erotic overtures. While Lorrie still found Max attractive, she claimed she was too "busy, tired, and stressed" to want lovemaking—and resented his "demands for sex." Their escalating fights over sexual issues masked other problems that were rooted in financial issues. Lorrie, the more successful partner, was tired of carrying the financial burden of their marriage. Under the circumstances, they had a difficult time settling on an initial Fantasy Encounter. He wanted to start with a Master/Slave scenario because he was anxious to give her pleasure, but she couldn't begin there.

"I already feel like a slave in real life," Lorrie said. They settled on a romantic Fantasy Encounter, "The Ultimate Seduction" (page 92), in which Max seduced her by plying her with compliments, gifts, and lavish attention over a period of several dates before making love to her. Their first week's Provocative Encounters picked up on that theme.

Lorrie insisted she was "too tired, stressed, and busy" to plan or participate actively in the Provocative Encounters, but she consented to let Max take charge of them. He chose to give her a series of massages, not touching her genitals until the third Encounter. "I understand that I have to take this very slowly with her," Max said. "I will be happy just to be allowed to hold and caress her for a change."

## The Provocative Encounter: The Basic Massage

Their first Provocative Encounter was a ten-minute body massage. Both Lorrie and Max dressed in comfortable, but attractive, T-shirts and underpants. Lorrie didn't wear a bra; and Max found her body very alluring. He whispered compliments in her ear as he massaged her back, shoulders, legs, arms, and stomach. Lorrie insisted he not massage her breasts or genitals in this Encounter. She didn't want to touch his genitals either.

The second Provocative Encounter was another clothed massage, but he was allowed to massage the tops of her breasts and her inner thighs. For the third Encounter, they were both naked. He caressed her breasts and genitals lightly, but he made no attempt to arouse her through manual stimulation and bring her to orgasm. She did become aroused.

For most couples, this first set of Encounters might feel

like baby steps. For Max and Lorrie, however, they were just the right pace.

## How the Provocative Encounter Worked

Lorrie and Max were both pleased with the Encounters. Their primary goal had been to help Lorrie feel relaxed about physical contact with Max, and they met that goal. They realized she would never feel desire for him until she could enjoy the physical sensations of being touched and held by him.

Lorrie said, "For the first time in years I didn't feel tense with him. I could relax and let him touch me, because I knew he wasn't going to push me for sex. I enjoyed his touch. The massage was pleasant at first, then exciting."

Max admitted that he was "disappointed at first" that their Encounters wouldn't include genital stimulation, but he was willing to do anything to make a fresh erotic start with his wife. "I was so used to her stiffening when I put my arms around her," he said. "It felt good to touch her without feeling her want to pull away. Before the third Encounter, she told me she was looking forward to it. That was gratifying and encouraging to me. I began to think we could make it after all."

After the first week, Lorrie was able to tell Max why she'd been so anxious about the Encounters: She was afraid their marriage would be over if she still felt no desire for him. Lorrie couldn't have let her defenses down and shared that with him if she hadn't felt "comfortable" during the Encounters and afterward. He was touched by her confession. Suddenly he saw her as vulnerable, not as cold and rejecting.

"The Provocative Encounters wouldn't have been possible for me if they weren't brief," Lorrie said. "The ten-minute time period was the key to success."

"The Basic Massage" is a good Provocative Encounter for couples like Lorrie and Max who have to overcome a history of anger, resentment, and emotional distance before they can reconnect sexually. A no-pressure massage is the least threatening way for them to reach out to each other again and rediscover each other's bodies without sexual expectations or pressures. But it's also a good Encounter to use when one partner is tired or stressed. For example, the partner who has just returned from an exhausting business trip or is involved in a difficult work or personal situation or recovering from an illness may not be able to respond to anything but a loving massage.

Most couples in the 21-Day Passion Fix program use some variation of "The Basic Massage" as their first Provocative Encounter in week one.

## *Arousal*

Arousal problems can be frustrating to a couple, in part, because many people confuse *arousal* and *desire*. If a man loses his erection during lovemaking, his partner often fears she isn't attractive to him or worries that he doesn't really desire her at all. When a woman has difficulty lubricating or becoming sufficiently aroused to reach orgasm, her partner often blames himself, too. And, he feels undesirable to his partner.

Arousal patterns change with age, physical and emotional condition, and even the age of the relationship. Women typically become aroused more easily as they move into their mid-thirties and through their forties—just as men begin having problems with arousal. Young men under thirty can get an erection on visual stimulation alone.

A thirty-five-year-old man who has been with the same partner for fifteen years may need more direct stimulation to his penis to get and maintain an erection than a man the same age who is in a new relationship.

## *The Couple*

Rachel desired her husband, John. He was the object of her frequent erotic fantasies, and she had no trouble describing the ways in which she found him physically attractive. Yet she rejected him sexually. When they came into my office, they were each feeling unappreciated and sexually rejected by the other.

Like many couples, John and Rachel had lost their close intimate connection in the lifestyle change accompanying parenthood. She gave up her career to stay home with their two small children. He didn't understand how difficult her life was. Each resented the other for not being passionate and romantic anymore. This couple had a sizzling courtship; each had been pursued by other admirers right up until the wedding. They revived that thrill of the chase in their first Fantasy Encounter, "The Voyeur" (page 97). John fantasized watching Rachel through a telescope making love with another man.

The Fantasy Encounter was titillating for both of them. After a few years of playing housewife and full-time mother, Rachel relished the idea of being desired by two men. They used the fantasy as mental foreplay for a week of Provocative Encounters designed to make her feel like the center of attention to his conquering romantic hero.

### The Provocative Encounter: Role-Playing a Roman Bacchanal

John and Rachel liked the idea of acting out fantasy roles. They settled on a Roman bacchanal, creating a scene reminiscent of Gladiator, a film they'd seen together and greatly enjoyed. John wrapped an animal-patterned bath towel around his waist in the fashion of a loincloth. Rachel wore a short one-shoulder white silk nightgown that resembled a toga and put a gardenia in her hair.

She sat in the middle of the bed with a bowl of grapes and a glass of wine. She was Roman royalty, a beautiful princess desired by many men; he was a gladiator who'd just won his freedom in a series of fights to the death. He initiated the Encounter by boldly sitting beside her and placing his hand on her leg—in full view of the (imaginary) banquet guests, including some of her lovers. When she laughed at his audacity and blushed at her sudden hot desire, he gave her a passionate kiss that took her by surprise. Within seconds, they had slipped their hands under each other's open clothing. In full view of the "audience," they masturbated each other to orgasm.

In the second and third Provocative Encounters that week, they continued to combine elements of exhibitionistic fantasy with manual and oral stimulation. For the second Encounter, Rachel played an expensive call girl who wanted John more than she'd ever wanted a man—and "serviced" him manually under the table in an expensive restaurant. In the third Encounter, John was a plumber who made her perform oral sex on him in the shower while her husband and several houseguests slept in nearby rooms.

## How the Provocative Encounter Worked

John was disappointed by the first Encounter because he'd wanted more than manual stimulation from Rachel. But he was pleased when she told him, "I'd forgotten how wonderful your kisses are." After the first Provocative Encounter, he noticed a significant change in her attitude toward him. "She's much more passionate about me," he said.

Rachel was a little disappointed in the Encounters because she'd wanted John to perform cunnilingus, but he insisted she "wait" until week two because he was afraid she wouldn't be satisfied with the experience. "I don't want to risk letting her down," he said. By the end of the week, they were both satisfied with the experiences—and the progress they'd made toward their sexual goal of increasing her arousal.

"We both realize how attractive we still find one another," she said. "We'd lost sight of that. After a week, we were talking more, saying nice things to each other, and laughing together again. I love feeling pursued by him."

Exhibitionist fantasies are arousing for most couples. They are particularly appealing to men and women who crave the excitement generated by the admiration of others. Some couples like to act out these fantasies in milder forms in semi-public places. They might, for example, pretend to be strangers meeting in a dark bar and move to a corner booth where they kiss and caress each other. Playing "footsies" under the table, dressing in revealing clothing on dates, and public displays of affection are really harmless but thrilling ways of behaving in a sexually exhibitionistic way.

## Technique: Manual Stimulation

**For Her**

- Apply a small amount of oil or sexual lubricant (such as Astroglide) to your fingertips.
- Stroke the outer and inner lips of her vulva in long, slow, sensual movements.
- If she is comfortable with this, insert a finger, or two, inside the vagina and locate the G spot and AFE zone. The G spot is a highly sensitive region beneath the vaginal lining along the urethra (the tube that the urine travels through as it exits the bladder) halfway between the pubic bone and the cervix. The AFE zone is a small, sensitive patch of rough feeling vaginal lining on the top wall of the vagina, closer to the cervix. Massaging the G spot assists in arousal, and stroking the AFE zone causes immediate lubrication in nearly all women.
- When she starts lubricating, run two fingers in the shape of a V along the sides of her clitoris.
- Using a light touch, move your fingers in a circular motion around the clitoris.
- Vary your strokes and rhythms and the amount of pressure applied as you circle and stroke the sides of the clitoris. Let her tell you if she wants direct pressure on the clitoris.

**For Him**

- Rub a small amount of oil or sexual lubricant into your hands.
- Grasp his penis at the base firmly, but not too firmly, in one hand.
- Stroke up and back down the shaft of his penis in a continuous smooth motion.
- Use your free hand to massage the head of the penis in a circular motion.
- Vary the pattern of stimulation by using different hand positions, including the "basket weave," a two-hand maneuver in which you lace your fingers together and place both hands around his penis.

*Chapter 12*

# Provocative Encounters to Pull You Out of a Sexual Rut

---

**The Problems:**
- Boredom
- Lack of variety
- Issues surrounding who initiates sex

---

**The Goals:**
- To alleviate boredom
- To add variety
- To change the sexual pattern
- To balance the erotic power

---

ONE OF THE MOST COMMON complaints among couples in long-term relationships is that the sex is boring. Some couples believe that sex inevitably becomes stale, tired, and routine after a couple has been together for years. Those expectations help create the problem. The couples stop trying to add variety to their lovemaking and soon have more excuses for sticking to the routine than they have positions and techniques in their sexual repertoire.

The feelings of comfort and safety that most people cherish in monogamous relationships can stifle erotic creativity—if they let that happen. Clients have often told me that they don't want to "upset" their partners by asking for sexual change. Sometimes they stay within the confines of the sexual routine because they don't want to risk their partner's disapproval or rejection if they ask for something different. Some men and women worry about looking foolish to their partners when they attempt a position or practice and don't make it work beautifully on the first try. So they don't try. Others won't break out of the rigid pattern of who initiates sex because they're afraid that would make them or their partners feel vulnerable and threatened.

These people are really just expressing a fear of changing the status quo in the relationship and risking the comfort and safety that sustains them. Change in any area of life can be difficult. But it's also exhilarating!

The 21-Day Passion Fix program makes it easy for couples to try new ways of making love. The brief duration of the Provocative Encounter encourages creative experimentation. Anyone can risk feeling uncomfortable or vulnerable for ten minutes.

Clients also tell me that the program worked for them in large part because they were able to implement it at home. "My wife and I tried weekend getaways and a Tantric sex workshop," one client said. "We failed miserably at reinventing our sex life under those circumstances. The pressure to perform was too intense. We would check into a hotel, look at each other, and silently panic. How were we going to fill a weekend with incredible lovemaking when we'd had sex maybe a half dozen times in the past year because we were bored with making love to each other?"

At the end of twenty-one days, that couple had revitalized their sex life. "The Provocative Encounters are the sexiest thing that ever happened to us," she said.

You're going to be saying the same thing soon.


# Boredom

Women's magazines frequently run cover lines promising to take the "boredom" out of sex. Most of the advice for doing that has also become boring and repetitious. Light candles, buy new lingerie, share a bubble bath, make a date for a romantic evening together, leave seductive notes and voice mails for each other. Therapists on television and radio talk shows dispense the same bromides. Any of these suggestions can be mildly beneficial to your sex life if doing them makes you feel more sensual and sexual.

But candles, flowers, love notes, and silk panties aren't going to make the sex sizzling. Provocative Encounters will.


## The Couple

Shelly and Adam defined their sexual problems differently. He blamed her sexual disinterest on low desire and difficulty reaching orgasm. She said, "I don't want to have sex because I'm bored with sex."

Adam took that comment as a personal attack on his abilities as a lover. Each accused the other of never wanting to "try something new." Finally they conceded that the issue was more complex: His idea of "something new" was more aggressive lovemaking, including occasional anal sex; she wanted to dress in provocative clothing, go to a club, and put on an exhibitionistic show with him on the dance floor. And she wanted more tenderness. How did they reconcile those seemingly divergent sexual desires?

In their initial Fantasy Encounter, "The Exhibitionist" (page 104), Shelly flaunted her sexuality on a dance floor, but Adam was the man who tamed the wild beauty and took her home where he made passionate love to her. The lovemaking combined the aggressive style he craved and the gentler one she wanted. Both were more aroused by the fantasy than they had believed possible. It was their impetus for developing Provocative Encounters that satisfactorily meshed their lovemaking styles.

## The Provocative Encounter: The Illicit Quickie

Shelly and Adam enthusiastically approached the third week of the 21-Day Passion Fix. In the first week, they had taken turns pleasing each other, with Adam playing the more dominant partner to restore his sense of confidence in himself as a lover. Shelly loved playing the role of the "sexual prize." In the second week, she indulged her exhibitionist fantasies by masturbating for him. Both felt they met their goals of more variety, increased arousal, and stronger desire.

By week three, they were ready for highly charged, aggressive lovemaking. She wanted to plan the first Encounter of that week as a Quickie in a restroom at a formal wedding reception. He balked at having sex in a bathroom stall where friends and relatives might discover them. They compromised: an "illicit" fully clothed Quickie at home in the last ten minutes before they had to be out the door headed for the reception.

Shelly wore a black low-cut dress that, Adam said, "snuggly fitted her curvy body. She'd never looked more sexy." He wore a black tuxedo. After exchanging compliments and admiring lusty glances, they kissed passionately. Adam unzipped his pants and told Shelly to kneel and perform fellatio. She did that just long enough to give him a solid erection. He talked about the details of their Fantasy Encounter, as she ministered to him, reminding her of how jealous the other men at the (imagined) club had been of him when he licked her breast as they danced.

Adam sat in a wide chair without arms. Shelly straddled him, facing him. He pushed her black-lace thong panties aside entered her, thrusting aggressively. When she was highly aroused, she got up, faced away from Adam, and sat down on him again. He continued thrusting deeply while stimulating her clitoris gently with his hand until she reached orgasm.

In their second Provocative Encounter that week, they also used a rear entry position. Again, he stimulated her clitoris as he thrust. By the third Encounter, she was ready and willing to satisfy Adam's desire and have anal sex with him.

"I did get highly aroused and it wasn't as uncomfortable as I'd feared it would be," she said. "Being totally submissive is an erotic thrill. Anal sex is not something I would do on a regular basis, but I'm willing to do it occasionally."

## How the Provocative Encounter Worked
The first encounter that week was extremely satisfying to

both Shelly and Adam. "I loved having sex while we were dressed up," Shelly said. "It felt naughty." Adam added, "We felt so good afterward that people kept coming up to us at the wedding reception and asking if we'd been to a spa resort or had lost weight or if Shelly was pregnant again. We were both glowing."

Their intense experience created even higher expectations for the second Provocative Encounter in this last week of their program—and they weren't disappointed. "We had the most tremendous simultaneous orgasm we ever experienced together," Shelly said. Adam added, "We started behaving differently toward one another. She was seductive and teasing."

Adam and Shelly felt they reached their goals of alleviating sexual boredom, taking risks sexually, and adding more spice and variety to their sex life by merging their differing sex styles. "At the beginning of the program, I hoped for some progress, but I didn't expect we'd come this far," Adam said. "Lack of time isn't even an issue anymore. When sex is more fun, there's always time for it."

## Technique: Anal Sex/Rear Entry

According to surveys, almost half of heterosexual couples (under age fifty) have tried anal sex at least once. Men are more likely than women to want a repeat performance, but some women do find occasional anal sex thrilling and satisfying. If you do it, be sure to:

- Use a specially designed anal condom to protect his urethra from bacteria

- Remove the condom before switching from anal to vaginal penetration
- Use copious amounts of a water-soluble lubricant, such as Astroglide
- Make sure she is very aroused before attempting penetration
- Make sure she relaxes the anal muscles
- Move slowly, at her pace, and penetrate only as deeply as she finds comfortable and acceptable

These alternatives to anal sex are almost like the real thing:

- *Make love in the rear entry position.* His penis is inserted in her vagina, not her anus, but the angle of penetration and the view of her buttocks make the experience different from intercourse in other positions.
- *Practice anal massage.* Using a thin latex glove finger and ample lubrication, circle the rim of your partner's anus, then insert your finger. Have your partner contract the anal muscle around your finger, inhaling as she/he does so. Release the muscle on the exhale.
- *Talk about anal sex, but don't do it.* If she's willing to talk him through the hottest anal sex scenario she can imagine—or borrow from a book or video—he may be satisfied with fantasy alone.
- *Combine rear entry intercourse and hot talk about anal sex.* Some women may find it easier to say, or hear, those words in this position because they aren't facing their partners. No eye contact, no embarrassment.

## *Variety*

Adding variety to the lovemaking routine should be the easiest sexual change a couple can make. But it isn't. Both men and women find introducing new ideas in the bedroom a difficult move. I've often heard clients say, "If I ask for something different, he [or she] will wonder where I got the idea. I don't want him [or her] to think I've been cheating." Here's another common excuse for staying in the same old rut: "My partner is too insecure [or uptight or rigid] to experiment with different practices or positions." Or "I don't want to do what he [or she] wants. That doesn't turn me on."

The subtext of many excuses is fear of failure. Men and women worry that the "something new" won't please their partners. It may even fail to live up to their expectations as well. If having sex were akin to performing brain surgery, trepidation would be understandable. Remind yourself that sex is supposed to be fun. This is one way that adults play. If that position you took from the Kama Sutra doesn't work, flip the pages and try another.

Sometimes couples cling to stale lovemaking patterns as if they were security blankets. They are! There's nothing wrong with wrapping yourself in the warmth of an erotic security blanket—just not every night.

### *The Couple*

Sharon and Larry, were coping with the sexual fallout from his treatment for prostate cancer when they came to see me. Still experiencing erectile difficulties, Larry avoided sex and considered any intimate contact with his wife a form of "pressure." He felt "old" and "inadequate," while she felt rejected by him. "He seems to think that there is no sex without his erection," Sharon said. "That means he doesn't have any interest in giving me pleasure."

They needed to redefine *sex* and add more variety to their lovemaking. As long as Larry equated "sex" with a reliable erection, he would continue avoiding sex. In the beginning, Sharon was more open to new ways of making love than he was. Their initial Fantasy Encounter, "The Eunuch Lover" (page 108), enabled him to play the observer watching Sharon be completely satisfied by her eunuch lover. Both were aroused imagining this skilled lover's ability to arouse her through his virtuoso oral and manual lovemaking techniques. In developing the story, Larry said, "I enjoyed playing a voyeur watching this exotic scene without feeling pressured to be part of it."

Afterward Larry admitted that he felt like the eunuch in the fantasy. He saw that, with or without an erect penis, a man could give a woman ultimate pleasure. And that realization freed him to become a lover with a varied repertoire. It's too bad that he didn't reach that conclusion without having to face erection problems related to illness and surgery.

## The Provocative Encounter: Masturbation

Sharon suggested that she take the lead in their first three Provocative Encounters in week one so Larry would continue to feel the same sense of "arousal without pressure" that he did during the Fantasy Encounter. In this first week, they set "more oral sex" as an immediate goal. They began with a ten-minute kiss. "I loved it!" Sharon said. "Kissing like that made me feel like we were dating again." Inspired by his "success" with her, Larry frequently complimented her over the next few days, making her feel sexually attractive for the first time in months. Their other two Encounters that week included oral stimulation of each other's bodies, including genitals, with no pressure for Larry to achieve erection. Sharon was lavish in her praise of his performance of cunnilingus, and that went a long way toward restoring his confidence in himself as a lover.

Their first Provocative Encounter in the second week was a daring and exciting one: Sharon masturbated for Larry. They drew on their Fantasy Encounter from week one, pretending that Larry was watching from the shadows as Sharon, who thought she was alone, pleasured herself. Wearing only a black silk tank top and thigh-high stockings, she sat up in bed, leaning back against the headboard, spread her legs wide, and positioned her body so that he would have a clear view of her genitals as she stroked and caressed herself. She threw her head back, closed her eyes, and gave herself over completely to the fantasy.

In their next Provocative Encounter, Larry masturbated as he watched her. When she became highly aroused, he stepped into her line of vision. Each continued masturbating with their eyes locked on each other. In the final encounter that week, they used mutual masturbation, side by side on the bed. Although Larry didn't get the kind of strong erection he dreamed of having, he did reach orgasm, his climax coinciding with her second one. In the third week, Sharon fulfilled one of his fantasies by allowing him to photograph her masturbating in one of their Provocative Encounters.

## How the Provocative Encounter Worked

Larry's primary personal sexual goal was reached in the first week of the Passion Fix program: He realized that he didn't need an erection to feel pleasure or give pleasure to his wife. "When I experienced pleasure even without an erection, I knew that I was going to be okay," he said. "That allowed me to concentrate on becoming a better lover."

Their masturbation Encounters were sexually liberating experiences for Sharon and Larry. Each felt they learned something new about their partners by watching each other perform this most intimate act. Sharon held and stroked Larry's penis the way he did. And he was "astonished" to discover what "nimble work with fingers" could do to arouse and satisfy her. Most important, they shed inhibitions.

Sharon said, "Larry's medical problem actually gave us the opportunity to be more daring and unconventional in our lovemaking. We had more excitement and passion in those three weeks than we'd had in the years prior to his illness. And Larry added, "If I hadn't experienced erection problems, we would still be making love in exactly the same way we'd been doing it for the last eighteen years. We might have ended up in separate beds out of boredom."

---

## Technique: Masturbating for Your Partner

- Create an enticing and erotic visual atmosphere through the use of lighting and costume. Use a position that shows your body to best advantage—as much for your confidence as your partner's arousal.
- Masturbate as part of a fantasy scenario. Role-playing

will help reduce anxiety. You'll shed inhibitions more easily as a "character" than as yourself.

- If you are too shy to make eye contact with your partner, pretend he or she is watching as a voyeur.
- But, do make eye contact if you can, especially at the moment of orgasm.
- In mutual masturbation, position yourselves side by side to feel closely connected—or at opposite ends of the bed to heighten the visual experience.

## Initiating Sex

Nothing shakes up the lovemaking routine like changing a rigid pattern of sexual initiation. If one partner typically initiates sex while the other holds veto power, both are likely to describe sex as "routine" or "boring." Each may accuse the other of being "rigid" or "inhibited" or "afraid of change." Almost inevitably, the initiator does not feel desired by his or her partner.

When that couple agreed to take turns initiating sex, they made something new and different happen immediately. Some couples will see the same kind of dramatic change when the refusing partner just stops saying no. There is no power in being the initiator if the other partner is more likely to reject the advance than accept it.

### The Couple
Jeff and Cindy were that "perfect couple," the one that

friends and acquaintances admire and envy. Attractive, intelligent, and personable, they related to each other in an easy, engaging way. They also had a thoroughly modern marriage in which she earned more money and he took greater responsibility for managing home and child care, especially during her frequent business trips. But they had one significant problem: They were seldom making love.

During most of their marriage, Jeff typically initiated sex. As her career heated up, Cindy more often than not rebuffed his advances, claiming she was "too tired" or "too busy" for sex. She defined their problem as "no time for sex." Jeff, on the other hand, believed she would make time for making love if she wanted him badly enough. "I'm tired of begging for sex," he said. "So I don't ask her often now."

They both agreed that Jeff needed to regain a sense of erotic power in the relationship. Cindy had exercised her right of sexual veto to the point where Jeff felt she was "in charge" of the sex, even when he played the dominant role. Their Fantasy Encounter, "The Film Director" (page 112), went a long way toward restoring his confidence in the sexual relationship. Jeff played a powerful director to Cindy's sexy starlet, who was eager to please him in every way. The fantasy thrilled her as much as it did him because she "finally was free of the responsibility of being in charge."

Their other sexual goals included adding variety to their lovemaking and keeping sexual desire alive while Cindy traveled.

### The Provocative Encounter: Sex Toy Play
Jeff and Cindy built on the success of their Fantasy Encounter by agreeing that he would plan and initiate the

Provocative Encounters throughout the program. "I need sex to be the place where I take direction, not give it," Cindy said. She promised not to resist Jeff's planned encounters if he would assure her that none of his ideas would be "offensive" to her.

Their first-week encounters included the use of fragrant lotions and oils in erotic body massages and very satisfying oral sex. The second week they faced the predictable obstacle: Cindy's travel schedule. They planned one Encounter in the wee hours of the morning before she had to leave for the airport, another in the shower on her return, and the third on the weekend while their son was visiting a friend. This final Provocative Encounter for the week combined elements of fantasy role-playing and vibrator play.

"In the fantasy," Jeff explained, "Cindy was having dinner with a girlfriend when she spotted me, the desirable stranger, dining with a woman. She followed me to the rest room and tried to pick me up, but I rejected her. Frustrated, she went home to masturbate—and that's where the vibrator came into play."

Jeff was completely in charge of the vibrator. Initially, he was intimidated by the idea of introducing a vibrator into their lovemaking, because he knew that Cindy pleasured herself with this tool, often while traveling. "I wanted him to use the vibrator on me, but I was afraid to ask," she said. "I didn't want him to be insulted.

Their "most incredibly successful" Provocative Encounter took place in the third week of the 21-Day Passion Fix program. Jeff purchased a strap-on vibrator, which allows a man to give his partner intense vaginal and clitoral stimulation as well as provide increased stimulation to his own genitals. He arranged for their son to stay with his grandparents, picked Cindy up from work, and told her the Provocative Encounter would begin as soon as they got home. He laid her on the kitchen counter and instructed her to arch her back and tilt her pelvis upward. With the help of the vibrator, he did the rest.

### How the Provocative Encounter Worked

Both Jeff and Cindy agreed that their sexual relationship began to improve in the first week of the program. To their surprise, so did the rest of their relationship. "I felt more in control of other areas of my life, not just the sexual parts," Jeff said. "And Cindy began to relax at home because she saw me as a strong person again. She'd let her bigger salary and the weight of her position at work carry over into our marriage. For that matter, so had I."

Incorporating sex toys into their lovemaking was Cindy's favorite part of their Encounters. "I loved the way Jeff used the vibrators to stimulate me," she said. "He gave me different sensations than I was able to give myself. I completely surrendered to pleasure. I loved the feeling that someone else was in charge; and I could depend on him to make it happen for me."

Their vibrator/intercourse Provocative Encounter gave them both strong, intense orgasms in a very short period. Tilting her pelvis by putting his hands under her buttocks and lifting up allowed Jeff to stimulate her G spot, an additional benefit. "I'd never felt like such a powerful lover," he said. And he added, "We certainly achieved our goal of adding variety to lovemaking."

The Provocative Encounters also helped them achieve

another goal: keeping desire alive across the miles. When Cindy traveled, they used their Fantasy Encounters to stimulate their desire for each other. They also talked about the Provocative Encounters in phone conversations. "Phone sex was a new experience for us," Cindy said. "It really keeps the erotic connection alive when we're not together."

## Technique: Playing with Sex Toys

The most commonly used sex toy is the vibrator, but it comes in a variety of sizes with an astonishing array of attachments. Other adult toys include dildos, feathers, various forms of restraints, ben wa balls (inserted into the vagina), penis rings, even whips, paddles, and clamps, the accoutrements of S/M. You can find these products in sex toy catalogues. (See page 153 for contact information.) They come with detailed instruction sheets.

To enhance vibrator play:

- Sustain the emotional connection by making eye contact, caressing, and kissing
- Experiment with different sizes, shapes, and attachments
- Use the vibrator as an erotic massage tool on other parts of the body, not just the genitals
- Combine penetration with the vibrator
- Don't limit the vibrator to use on her (She can use it on him, too. For example, she can strap a small vibrator to the back of her hand as she performs manual stimulation on his penis.)

*Chapter 13*

## *Provocative Encounters to Intensify Sex*

---

**The Problems:**
- Performance anxiety
- Performance difficulties
- Poor erotic technique
- Difficulty reaching orgasm

---

**The Goals:**
- To reduce performance anxiety and improve performance
- To improve technique
- To increase frequency of orgasm
- To increase orgasmic potential

---

MANY COUPLES who say they have "no time" or "no energy" for sex would make the time and find the energy if they and their partners were better lovers. Yes, they're probably busy and stressed—who isn't?—but they're also using those excuses to avoid facing their real problem: poor technique. When partners

190

don't know how to arouse and please each other, they are more likely to have orgasm difficulties and performance anxieties. In every other area of life, people assume that they need to develop good skills to assure a positive outcome. No one expects to get a job without qualifications, dance an elegant tango without a few lessons, or cook a gourmet meal without recipes.

Yet many couples believe that great sex should naturally flow from emotional intimacy and an erection. When it doesn't, they lament the "lack of passion." Despite all the information available on women's orgasms, a lot of women, and men too, still believe she can have—or he can "give" her—bed-quaking orgasms on the strength of "passion" and a good erection alone. Some women fail to reach orgasm with proficient lovers because emotional or psychological issues prevent them from letting go. Most women, however, fail to reach orgasm because they aren't getting the kind of clitoral stimulation they need when they need it.

In truth, passion fades if sex fails to produce exciting results, at least some of the time. Technique is important. While technique alone isn't sufficient to sustain a passionate relationship, neither are feelings. That's the message missing in so much modern relationship advice like a never-ending tape loop of a Barbara Streisand song about feelings, feelings, feelings.

The 21-Day Passion Fix program is different because it fixes the sex first. Have good sex. The feelings will follow.

When a couple who has a basically good relationship learns how to make love better, the relationship improves, sometimes as dramatically as their sex life does. Their feelings of love and passion intensify as they become more skilled at arousing and satisfying each other. Provocative Encounters aimed at improving lovemaking skills help couples connect physically and emotionally.

## Performance Anxiety

Traditionally, performance anxiety has been regarded as a male-only problem. The very definition was rooted in his erection. When a man could not "perform" by getting and maintaining an erection, he became anxious. Increasingly, women have performance anxiety, too. They feel the pressure to be "good" in bed, especially as they, and their relationship, age. Being attractive isn't enough anymore. A woman also needs to have her own erotic bag of tricks to remain a desirable sex partner. Now either partner may feel anxious about ability to "perform" in bed.

Either partner's anxiety can inhibit lovemaking, but sex typically will go on if she, not he, is the one worrying about how she's doing. His concerns about his erections are more likely to limit how often they make love. He won't want to risk failure; and she might not want to put pressure on him by initiating sex. Some men develop performance anxiety after they've failed on a few occasions to achieve an erection or sustain one during lovemaking. Their fear becomes a self-fulfilling prophecy. Because they think they're going to have erection problems, they do. And continued "failures" create a circle of disappointment and avoidance for both partners.

You can't be a passionate lover if you're self-conscious about your performance—or if you're in bed with someone who can't get past his or her own insecurities.

## The Couple

Peter only consented to seek help for his sexual problems because his live-in girlfriend, Angela, left him little choice. Both in their early thirties, they'd been living together for only two years when they came to see me. He was embarrassed about seeking help. Like many people, he bought into the myth of the hot young couple. They were young and hadn't been together long enough for the passion to fade; and he was ashamed to admit they weren't hot.

He blamed his erectile difficulties on "trying too hard" to please Angela, the more sexually experienced of the two. She didn't understand why he either lost his erection or ejaculated too quickly when they were making love. And she certainly didn't consider herself "demanding" when she asked him to act out her bondage fantasies. Peter insisted that he was a "gentle, caring lover" who couldn't "see" himself in a dominant sexual role. Neither one was optimistic about resolving the sexual differences.

But they began to make real headway when they discussed their first Fantasy Encounter, "Erotic Bondage" (see page 118). Peter suddenly understood that the dichotomy of being nice outside the bedroom and quite the opposite sexually was very exciting to Angela. She loved his behavior as a gentle, considerate boyfriend. But she still wanted him to be masterful in the bedroom.

Their Provocative Encounters were designed to give him the more aggressive role. He was able to become the initiator because his anxiety was greatly reduced by the prohibition against intercourse in the first week of the program. Peter and Angela acted out different versions of their bondage fantasy in the Provocative Encounters, with Peter playing the dominant role. By the second week, he felt equal to Angela as a lover. Confident of his ability to arouse and please her, Peter was ready to be more creative in designing the Provocative Encounters.

### The Provocative Encounter: The Blindfold Game

As the first and third Provocative Encounters in the second week, Peter and Angela played a variation of the Blindfold Game. Angela didn't know what Peter was going to do to her. He planned the Encounters, including shopping for the props. They agreed that he would arouse her and bring her to orgasm, but how he did that was entirely up to him as long as each event was different. Intercourse was an option, but not a requirement.

After they'd agreed to play the game, Angela found the idea of being bound and blindfolded so exciting that she "couldn't stop fantasizing about it." She was confident Peter would keep his promise to bring her to orgasm each time. After his successes in the first week, Peter was eager to play the role of conquering lover, especially since Angela wouldn't be able to see if he sustained an erection or not.

Peter bought her a frilly satin sleep mask as a blindfold. She dressed in an alluring blouse and skirt that he could easily "rip" from her body and a wispy lace thong. He tied her wrists to the bedposts, blindfolded her, and told her she was his captive. When she begged to be released—part of the script—he pulled open her blouse, roughly pushed her skirt up around her waist, and ran his hands all over her exposed flesh. He licked and sucked her nipples, sometimes biting them gently.

Using velvet and silk scarves to cover his hands, he teased her by stroking and fondling her breasts and thighs, varying the strength of his touch, until she was aroused.

In the first Provocative Encounter, he used a vibrator, surprising her by running it along parts of her body she hadn't considered sensitive to electric stimulation, including the backs of her knees. He brought her to orgasm with the vibrator. But in the third Provocative Encounter that week, Peter had a different "grand finale": intercourse. He used the vibrator to arouse her quickly. Then he pulled off her lace thong and entered her. Angela reached orgasm before Peter did.

### How the Provocative Encounter Worked

Angela and Peter both felt their Fantasy Encounters helped make the Blindfold Game as successful as it was. Angela quickly learned to use fantasy to arouse herself in advance of lovemaking. Peter said, "The Fantasy Encounters helped me practice new techniques in my head, before trying them out with Angela. I could fantasize her excitement, and I was expecting her to respond that way. I didn't worry about how she would respond. There was no hesitation, no time lost in measuring how I was affecting her."

That Angela couldn't see his erection during the Encounter also helped him. "I didn't have to worry about whether I lost it or not," Peter said. "I only had to please her. I felt free." He was able to discover his own repressed erotic desires because he was no longer monitoring his performance.

According to Angela, Peter became a "different man" when he made love to her while she was blindfolded. "I didn't know where he was going to touch me next or how he would touch me," she said. "That was very exciting. The anticipation made me feel tingly all over my body. He was in control. And he was my fantasy lover come to life."

By the beginning of week three, Peter had almost no performance anxiety. He'd learned new sexual techniques and was confident of his ability to satisfy his lover, erection or not. He even joked that having erection and ejaculatory problems was the "best thing" for their sex life. "That gave me the motivation to learn new techniques," he said. "If I hadn't had any problems, I would have gone along being an adequate lover."

## Technique: Blindfold Sex

- Tie the blindfold loosely. And take turns being the blindfolded partner.
- Explore the sense of touch by stroking the submissive partner's body with different fabrics, feathers, or even unusual objects like a feather duster or a bath sponge.
- Experiment with different kinds of touch, from lightly touching with only the pads of your fingertips, like a spider walking, to more firm caresses as arousal grows.
- Don't move in a predictable pattern. Not knowing where you will be kissed, touched, or caressed next heightens the excitement.
- Remember the other senses. Talk sexy. Consider introducing erotic foods, such as strawberries, whipped cream, and chocolate, into the game.

## *Technique*

Many couples go along being merely adequate lovers because no dramatic problem makes them take stock and change the erotic status quo. They may have been inexperienced lovers or sexually inhibited when they got together and just accepted each other's lack of lovemaking skill as the best they could hope to have. Or, they may have been good lovers once, but stopped trying long ago.

Men and women have many excuses for not learning new sex techniques. Often they blame their partner who would, they're convinced, "not like" any change in the erotic routine. Sometimes that partner is secretly longing for change but doesn't know how to introduce the idea.

As long as these couples aren't confronted with his erection difficulties, they may not acknowledge having a problem. "We don't have sex very often, but when we do, it works fine," they tell each other. If it worked better, they would have sex more often.

### *The Couple*

Sophie was angry with her boyfriend, Frank, when she "dragged" him into therapy. "He doesn't know how to please me," she said. Later she admitted, "I feel sexually unattractive to him because he doesn't try to please me. If he really wanted me, he would try harder." Because he didn't "try harder," Sophie was having an increasingly difficult time getting aroused when they did make love.

For his part, Frank found Sophie "critical and demanding."

He said, "She can't be pleased," but added, "I don't know how to give her what she wants in bed," in a softer voice.

Both in their late thirties, Frank and Sophie had reached a relationship impasse neither had confidence they could cross. Initially both expressed doubt that a twenty-one-day program could turn their sex life around. They considered Fantasy Encounters "a silly exercise." But, their first Fantasy Encounter, "The Genie in the Bottle" (see page 125), helped them both make progress toward their sexual goals of improving Frank's technique and meeting Sophie's need for more excitement and greater variety.

They discovered they loved role-playing. Both felt they could improve sexual communication by assuming fantasy roles. "Talking about sex is less threatening this way," Sophie said. They built their Provocative Encounters around this concept.

## The Provocative Encounter: Oral Sex

Sophie and Frank enlivened their first week's Provocative Encounters by incorporating sexy dialogue into their erotic massages. They took turns playing roles like the massage parlor prostitute or the masseur pretending to be gay so he could take liberties while massaging his "client." They particularly liked two aspects of these Encounters: the play-acting and the concept of "taking turns pleasing one another." In the second week, they planned one oral sex Provocative Encounter to please her and another for him. The third Encounter was mutual masturbation.

Frank chose a role for the cunnilingus Encounter that allowed him to be the experienced lover to her ingénue. She was a young, sexually inexperienced woman who had yet to experience orgasm with a partner. He was the sophisticated European who met, and conquered her, in the first-class cabin on a flight from New York City to London. Sitting in the next seat, he moved from intimate chat to putting a hand in her lap. More excited by him than she'd ever been by any man, she wriggled nervously in her seat. He suggested they meet in the bathroom. In real time, Sophie and Frank did meet in the bathroom. She sat on the vanity chair while he performed cunnilingus, giving her not one but two orgasms.

In the fellatio Encounter, Sophie pretended to be an ambitious, star-struck Washington intern to Frank's powerful politician. He sat at his desk in the study and pretended to ignore her efforts to engage his erotic attention. She unbuttoned her blouse a bit, sat on the edge of his desk, and seductively crossed her legs clad in sheer black stockings. Though he feigned indifference, she looked down and saw his erection, obvious in his fitted trousers. She pushed back his chair, sank to her knees, unzipped his pants, and performed fellatio. His orgasm, she said, "was almost as thrilling to me as it was to him."

## How the Provocative Encounter Worked

Treating sex as an even exchange helped put this couple on equal sexual terms for the first time in their relationship. That was important to both Frank and Sophie. He needed the confidence in his lovemaking abilities; and she needed to feel he desired making love to her as much as she did to him.

Their first oral Provocative Encounter, cunnilingus, was arousing to both of them. "She had strong orgasms, and I felt like a god," Frank reported. "Focusing attention solely on pleasing Sophie helped me develop technique," he added. The fellatio Encounter was equally successful for both partners. "We learned more about each other's sexuality in those encounters," she said.

At the end of the program, Sophie and Frank did say they found it difficult to make the transition from expressing their sexual desires as "characters" to making requests as themselves. "That was the hard part," Sophie said, "but we did it. When we feel shy or awkward about speaking as ourselves, we know we can say, 'Pretend I am so-and-so and this is what I want.' The role-playing will ease the way for us."

## Technique: Oral Stimulation

### Cunnilingus

- Be sure that both partners are in a comfortable position, typically the woman lying on her back with her legs drawn up and spread, the man lying between her legs, with his arms under her legs, his hands gently supporting her buttocks.

- Become proficient at the basic strokes: flick, lick, and suck. Flick your tongue lightly across the tip of the clitoris and the shaft. Lick the tip of your tongue in long and short strokes from the labia minora to the tip of the clitoris. Suck the clitoris by placing your lips on either side of it and gently pulling in.

- Use a combination of the strokes. Also, vary the pressure and speed of flicking, licking, and sucking.

- Add manual stimulation. Use your fingers to stimulate her vagina as you perform cunnilingus.
- To give her multiple orgasms, continue the stimulation after the first orgasm. If she is too sensitive for direct clitoral stimulation, shift your attention to the sides of the clitoris and the vaginal lips.

## Fellatio

- Get into a comfortable position. An easy position for both partners is this one: He lies on his back. She kneels at his side, her knees at right angles to his hip.
- Hold his penis firmly, but don't squeeze it. Fondle his testicles occasionally as you perform fellatio.
- Become proficient at the basic strokes: flick, lick, and suck. Flick the head of the penis quickly with the tip of your tongue, and flick up and down the shaft. Use swirling licks around the head of the penis. Lick in long strokes up the shaft. Suck the head of the penis, gently.
- Pay special attention to his hot spots: the head of the penis; the corona, or ridge separating the head from the shaft; and the frenulum, the loose section of skin running from the edge of the coronal ridge to the beginning of the shaft.
- Use a combination of the strokes. Vary the pressure and speed of flicking, licking, and sucking.
- To prolong fellatio, take your mouth away from his penis when he is close to ejaculating and lick his scrotum or thighs or lightly bite his nipples.

## The Second Couple

Technique was the issue for newlyweds Sam, thirty-three, and Nina, twenty-eight. They came to see me because Sam was having difficulty maintaining an erection during intercourse. But his problem was not performance anxiety. He needed more, and more skillful, fellatio to get him aroused for intercourse than Nina knew how to provide.

"I'm not that aroused when we begin intercourse," Sam finally admitted. "That's the real problem. She licks me a few times and quits."

Nina didn't like performing fellatio for two reasons: She knew she wasn't good at it, and she was afraid that Sam would ejaculate in her mouth. Both her concerns could be addressed by improved skills. Once she became adept at fellatio, she could gauge his level of arousal and trust that he would pull back before ejaculation.

Sam needed to improve his lovemaking skills, too. Because Nina had been "too shy" to allow him to perform cunnilingus on her very often, he said he "didn't put the energy into being a good lover" that he had with previous partners. Compounding their problems, each was sensitive to criticism and "rejection."

Sam and Nina were two highly competitive people who didn't have trouble taking constructive criticism in other areas of their lives. That indicated they could learn to talk about improving sexual technique, too. I helped them find a way to use their competitiveness as a vehicle for improving lovemaking. They also used "The Genie in the Bottle" (see page 125) as one of their Fantasy Encounters. Nina played the genie. She loved the sense of erotic power this fantasy gave her over Sam. Fantasizing driving him wild with fellatio was all the incentive she needed to learn how to—and to believe she could—do it in real life. Sam also wanted to seize the erotic power. They developed Provocative Encounters that enabled them to feel like skilled lovers capable of leaving each other gasping in delight.

### The Provocative Encounter: The Erotic Competition

In the first week of the 21-Day Passion Fix program, Sam and Nina created Provocative Encounters that focused on passionate kissing, fellatio, and cunnilingus. They accomplished their primary goal of the week: improving kissing and other oral skills. By the second week, they were ready to indulge their competitive instincts and further improve their oral techniques while making intercourse more exciting.

Their first and second Provocative Encounters that week were erotic contests. "We were erotic urban guerrillas," he said, laughing. "We pretended to be the most sexually skilled man and woman in the modern arena; and we were in a contest to see who was ultimately better."

Sam challenged Nina to bring him to orgasm in less time than he could bring her to orgasm. In the first Encounter, they were limited to using oral and manual skills only. Nina won that contest by bringing Sam to orgasm through fellatio faster than he could bring her to orgasm by cunnilingus. The second Encounter was an intercourse Quickie staged in the kitchen. Fully dressed except for underwear, they took turns providing oral stimulation. Sam hoisted Nina up on the kitchen counter, and they had intercourse in this position. Because Nina was highly aroused and he was able to penetrate deeply, she reached orgasm seconds before he did.

"Hard to say who really won that contest," Sam joked. "It was almost a tie.

### How the Provocative Encounter Worked

Their success with the first week's Provocative Encounters allowed Sam and Nina to be more playful, daring, and creative in the second week. She was especially happy to realize she could arouse Sam through fellatio. Once she had that success, she really enjoyed performing fellatio. And, she was able to relax and let Sam please her orally, too.

The Erotic Competition inspired them to work quickly at mastering new lovemaking techniques. But there were other benefits to the game. Competing turned sex from a serious business into adult play. Sam was too involved in the competition to worry about losing his erection. Nina forgot her self-consciousness and threw herself into "winning."

They had so much fun trying to be "the better lover" that they felt emotionally closer than they had since the early days of their courtship.

## Orgasms

A woman's orgasm isn't optional anymore. It's a necessary component of lovemaking. Even women who say they don't "always have to come" to enjoy sex admit that they do expect to experience orgasm at least some, or most, of the time. Men measure their abilities as a lover by whether their partners have one or multiple orgasms.

Despite the emphasis on the female orgasm, many couples don't know how to ensure that she does have one. Only about one-third of women reach orgasm via intercourse alone, no matter the size of his penis or the duration of his erection. For the majority of women, additional clitoral stimulation, typically in the form of manual stroking, is necessary to reach orgasm during intercourse. Yet many women find it hard to ask for the stimulation they need—and are too embarrassed to touch themselves.

Some couples skirt the issue by him giving her an orgasm via cunnilingus before intercourse. That's fine. But having an orgasm during intercourse is right at the fingertips, either his or hers. Why not have it both ways?

### The Couple

Laura, fifty-two, was a reluctant client, but her husband of four years, Gary, forty, insisted they seek help for her problem. Laura had never experienced an orgasm, either alone or with a partner. She said she didn't care about having an orgasm and blamed his desire to give her one on "his ego." He was frustrated by his inability to satisfy her. Not surprisingly, they seldom had sex.

In developing their first Fantasy Encounter, "Playing Doctor" (see page 128), Laura surprised both of them with her sexual creativity. In the Fantasy, she played an actress in a medical drama, paralyzed from the waist down. Gary was the doctor who restored her sensations through sensual massage, culminating in orgasm.

The Fantasy worked on several levels. First, Laura began to experience herself as a sexual person. She saw Gary as someone who really could take care of her erotic needs if she surrendered herself to his lovemaking. And Gary began to believe that "someday she would have an orgasm," which finally allowed him to relax.

But Laura was still reluctant to try the Provocative Encounters. "I don't like the idea of scheduled sex," she said. "My schedule is too crowded already." Gary countered by saying, "Do you mean that we aren't as important to you as everything else in your life?" Then she admitted that she was afraid "real sex" wouldn't live up to her "doctor fantasy."

"What if I still haven't had an orgasm when the program is over?" Laura asked. "Will Gary be disappointed in me?" He said he would only be disappointed if she didn't try. They agreed to make the Provocative Encounters "priority appointments" to be rescheduled immediately if cancellation became necessary.

## The Provocative Encounter: The Spin Cycle Quickie

In the first week, their Provocative Encounters included different methods of oral and manual stimulation. Gary used his good sense of humor to lighten the sexual tension between them. And they agreed not to define success in orgasm terms. If Laura felt more pleasure than anxiety, they deemed the Encounter a success. By the second week, they said their lovemaking was already more playful, less stressful, and "much more fun."

They integrated two vibrators into their lovemaking during

the second week. A wand vibrator with attachments and a small palm-sized vibrator were Laura's introduction to sex toys. She was surprised to experience her first orgasm via vibrator stimulation. The only drawback for her was a lingering sense that she "should" have had an orgasm with Gary, not with an "electric toy."

That inspired Gary to develop the "Spin Cycle Quickie" as their first Provocative Encounter in week three. He "surprised" Laura while she was doing the laundry by grabbing her from behind and nuzzling her neck as his hands roamed up and down the front of her body. When she moaned in pleasure, he turned her around, kissed her passionately, and ground his pelvis against hers. Then he picked her up and put her on top of the washing machine, spread her legs, took off her underpants, and alternated stimulating her genitals with his mouth and hand. When the machine kicked into the spin cycle, he unzipped his pants and had intercourse with Laura from his standing position. She had an intense orgasm.

## How the Provocative Encounter Worked

The combination of sensations created by the vibrating machine and Gary's skilled lovemaking gave Laura the kind of orgasm she'd never really believed she would have. "I was stunned by the intensity," she said. "Whenever I'd read about the earth moving and all that jazz, I didn't believe it. Now I do."

That Encounter helped her see herself in a new way. "I am a sexy woman," Laura said. "I never knew that about me."

Her orgasm also made Gary feel better about himself. "This is what I wanted to give her," he said. "I fantasized about making her feel this way."

An unanticipated extra bonus to the Spin Cycle Quickie: Gary is more willing to help with the laundry. "We aren't fighting about the chores all the time," Laura laughed. "Who knew doing laundry could be so much fun?"

---

### Technique: Her Orgasm

- Don't use "I don't need an orgasm" as an excuse for not trying to have one. Accept responsibility for your own orgasm. You need to show and tell him what to do.
- Experiment with intercourse positions to find the ones most conducive to orgasm. Many women find female superior position the best orgasm position because they control the angle and penetration of thrusting. His hands are free to provide additional clitoral stimulation.
- Do not be afraid to ask for that extra stimulation.
- Feel free to touch yourself during lovemaking. He will probably find that arousing, not threatening.
- Tone your pubococcygeal (PC) muscles, the muscles in the vaginal floor. (Locate them by squeezing to stop and start the flow of urine.) Flexing those muscles can encourage and strengthen orgasms. The following exercises, called Kegels, can get your PC muscles in shape. You can do them while standing in line, driving, or lying on the sofa watching TV.
  - *A short Kegel squeeze.* Contract the PC muscles twenty times at approximately one squeeze per second. Do two sessions a day twice a day. Gradually build up to two sets of seventy-five per day. Then add:

- *A long Kegel squeeze.* Hold the muscle contraction for a count of three. Relax between contractions. Work up to holding for ten seconds, relaxing for ten seconds. Again, start with two sets of twenty each and build up to seventy-five.
- When you're doing 300 sets a day, 150 each of the short and long, add:
- *The Kegel push-out.* After releasing the contraction, push down and out gently, as if you were having a bowel movement with your PC muscles. Repeat: gently. No bearing down. Now create:
- *Kegel sequences.* Combine long and short repetitions with push-outs in any pattern you like. Do 300 sets a day. After two months of daily sets of 300, you should have well-developed PC muscles. You'll notice the difference in how your orgasms feel. And, you'll be able to grasp his penis with your muscles during intercourse, increasing his arousal and strengthening his orgasm, too.
- You can maintain that condition simply by doing 150 sets a day, several days a week.

*Chapter 14*

# Provocative Encounters to Enhance Intimacy

---

**The Problems:**
- Poor communication skills, especially sexual communication
- Lack of closeness in the relationship
- General sense of not feeling connected to each other

**The Goals:**
- To improve sexual communication
- To elicit a dialogue about the sexual relationship
- To enhance intimacy
- To restore feelings of closeness and affection toward each other

---

MEN AND WOMEN don't always agree on what constitutes "intimacy" in a relationship. Men are likely to say that love-making *is* intimacy, while women define intimacy as "talking about feelings." If he's a caring lover and a faithful partner who brings her tea in bed when she's sick with the flu, he doesn't understand why she needs to have talks about "feelings," too. More than one male client has asked me: "Why do I have to talk about how I feel when I'm showing her how I feel?" Inevitably his partner insists: "He never talks. How can I know what he's feeling when he won't open up to me?"

All you need to do to comprehend the emotional difference between men and women is look at the way they behave in a common situation, the breakup of a friend's relationship. She fills her bag with tissues and takes her friend out for a glass of wine and a tearful, cathartic release of the torrent of feelings. He takes his buddy to a sporting event. Afterward they eat and drink, but they don't talk about his feelings.

Men and women have been socialized to express their emotions in different ways. He thinks frequent lovemaking maintains an intimate relationship just as he thinks that doing something active with his friend is a way of showing his support in a difficult time. She thinks emotional conversations sustain the connection between lovers and friends. In the past two decades, "her" viewpoint gained cultural ascendancy over his, in part through the popularity of talk shows and self-help books, largely aimed at women and, not surprisingly, telling women exactly what they wanted to hear.

I don't do that. Therapy should *not* be the place where women drag their men to hear the message that the woman is right. The 21-Day Passion Fix program works because it recognizes the value of both perspectives: his and hers.

He is more likely to express his feelings to her after lovemaking. The more often they make love, the more likely he will "open up" in the way she wants him to do. And, the more satisfying the sex is for her, the more willing, even eager, she will be to make love as often as he wants.

Emotional intimacy in a sexual relationship is sustained by the sex.

## Communication

Most couples know that good "communication" is important in an intimate relationship. But there's more to communicating than expressing your own feelings without regard to how your expressions will affect your partner. A good communicator also speaks tactfully and listens carefully. In addition to these two components of communicating—listening and talking—there is a third: nonverbal expression. During lovemaking, moaning, sighing, gasping, screaming, and guiding a partner's hand or mouth to the desired place are often more meaningful communiqués than conversation.

When lovemaking isn't satisfactory, however, couples need to talk about it, preferably outside the bedroom. Talking honestly about sex may be more difficult than speaking the truth to each other about almost anything else. There are many ways to dissemble about sexual needs and desires—and so many excuses for not being straightforward. A faked orgasm, for example, is a kind of lie. The motive may be altruistic—to make him feel good—but the end result is perpetuating a style of lovemaking that won't lead to orgasm for her.

Couples who "never talk" anymore probably don't have sex very often either. They may lie to each other about sex. And they probably say, "*You* don't do this in bed," when they should say, "*I* want to make love this way." *You* is accusatory. *I* takes responsibility for making the sex better.

## *The Couple*

Ilene, fifty-two, and Ron, fifty-six, had just faced one significant milestone, their twentieth wedding anniversary, and were approaching another, the empty nest, when they came to see me. He was bored with their sex life. She felt threatened when he said that. He wanted her to initiate sex more often and, especially, to "participate more actively, by telling me what she likes, what she wants, and how I make her feel. She's so quiet in bed, I don't know if she's excited or not."

Ilene insisted that she enjoyed their sexual relationship, though she wasn't the "noisy" type. But she did realize that she had to make changes "to make Ron happy." She was, she admitted tearfully, afraid of losing him if she didn't.

While she agreed to participate fully in the program with him, she was too inhibited to help develop their initial Fantasy Encounter, "An Erotic Fairy Tale" (see page 134). She did find the fantasy arousing. Their Provocative Encounters that week focused on telling each other how the oral and manual stimulation felt. *Ilene* wasn't able to tell Ron how she felt as he was stimulating her. But she did begin to open up during their afterplay period as Ron held her, gently hugging and kissing her.

The first week of the program was difficult for Ilene, because meeting her sexual goal, becoming more sexually expressive and responsive, required significant change on her part. "I feel anxious," she said as she entered the second week. "I see benefits to Ron, to our marriage, especially our sex life, but this is hard."

Ilene learned something important about herself in the first week of the program: She had fallen into the habit of "using intercourse" to hurry lovemaking to a conclusion whenever Ron's oral or manual "foreplay" made her uncomfortable or anxious. "I would pull him on top of me to have intercourse to avoid doing whatever I didn't want him to do," she said. "He would ejaculate fairly quickly and fall asleep. Since we couldn't have intercourse in the first week of the program, I couldn't hide behind that behavior."

The first week was difficult for Ron, too. He had to curb his impatience at what seemed like her "slow progress" to him. The absence of intercourse left him "feeling like a high school kid ready to explode." He was ready for hotter Encounters. She pushed herself through her anxiety to participate more actively in the second week; and she made significant progress toward her goals. By the end of that week, she could tell Ron in more detail what she did and didn't like about their Provocative Encounters.

## The Provocative Encounter: The Tantric Position

Ron developed the Provocative Encounters in weeks one and two. They agreed that Ilene would be in charge of planning one Encounter in the third week. The time was set, of course, but the nature of the Encounter was to be Ilene's "surprise." From a book on Tantric sex, she chose an intercourse position, the Yab-yum.

"One of Ron's goals was adding variety, including new positions, to lovemaking," Ilene said. "He complained that we used the missionary position too often, and he was right. We did. I wanted to please him by choosing a new intercourse position, but I also pleased myself by selecting something that appealed to me."

On the night of their Encounter, Ilene told Ron to undress

and sit in the middle of their bed. Wearing only a short silk robe, she stroked his penis and fondled his testicles until he had an erection. Then she slipped out of the robe and sat on the bed, facing him. She instructed him to look deeply into her eyes as she guided him into position. Their eyes locked; they stroked each other's backs, kissed with their eyes open, and regulated their breathing together.

Ron wanted to penetrate her immediately, but Ilene made him wait until she felt intensely excited by this new kind of foreplay. When she was ready, she guided his penis inside her. The pressure she felt against her clitoris was thrilling. She controlled the speed of movement as they rocked together, rubbing each other's backs, and kissing at the same time. They each experienced an intense orgasm.

## How the Provocative Encounter Worked

From the beginning of the program, Ilene insisted that she would determine the "expressions of pleasure" she would use during lovemaking. "Loud cries and moans are not my style," she said. "I told Ron I would let him know when I am enjoying what he's doing by smiling at him and I would tense my body to indicate I was highly aroused and near orgasm."

Ron accepted her conditions of expression, and Ilene immediately began to enjoy lovemaking more because she felt less pressured "to emote." After the first week, she could talk with him about the Provocative Encounters without feeling embarrassed. As their sexual communication improved, they felt more emotionally connected, too.

The Yab-yum Encounter was successful for both of them. Ilene liked the gentle and intimate nature of the lovemaking.

"I like having eyes open during lovemaking," she said. "Looking into Ron's eyes, I can help him know what I'm feeling." Ron said, "I was thrilled to have her come to me with a new intercourse position. She was the teacher. That was very arousing."

Their Provocative Encounters, particularly this one, taught Ron and Ilene that they could have "great sex in a short time period." Ron said, "I don't think we would have been able to handle a program that required us to make love for long periods of time. One, we don't have that kind of time. And, two, Ilene would have been too intimidated to try."

Their improved sexual communication also led to better communication in general. In their afterplay following the Yab-yum Encounter, Ron told Ilene he'd been terrified of being a middle-aged man trapped in a boring life. She understood why he needed to make their sex life more exciting. "It's about him, not just me," she said. They agreed that adding more variety to their sex life would be the beginning of change in other areas of their life together, too. "We want to listen to new music, see foreign films, expand our social circle, and travel more widely," she said.

"I don't feel old anymore," Ron said.

## The Yab-yum

- Sit in the center of the bed facing each other. Look deeply into each other's eyes as you caress each other. Hold the look. This is called the eye lock. You probably won't realize how little you do look into each other's eyes during lovemaking until you practice the eye lock.

- Wrap your legs loosely around each other so she is "sitting" on his legs, his erection between your bodies. Place your right hand at the back of your partner's neck, your left hand on your partner's tailbone.
- Press your palm firmly at the base of your partner's spine. Slide your hand up his or her back to the back of the neck, and then to the top of the head. Imagine you are channeling sexual energy up through the body, warming the body from the genitals through the heart to the head. Repeat the stroke over and over again until you are both feeling very aroused.
- Insert his penis into her vagina so that the shaft exerts as much indirect pressure as possible on her clitoris. Rock slowly together as you rub each other's back and perform the eye lock.
- Move together faster and harder as arousal increases.

## *Intimacy*

Though they express their needs and emotions in different ways, both men and women crave a deep, intimate connection within a sexual relationship. That relationship is the place where they can be themselves emotionally and sexually and express themselves verbally and physically without being judged. For men, this relationship may be the only place where he feels safe enough to risk the vulnerability that accompanies emotional exposure. For women, this relationship may be the only place where she feels safe enough to be freely sexual. The stakes are high for both.

Women typically complain that men are "afraid" of intimacy or "don't know how" to be intimate. They want more time and attention, and more talking, from their men who, they complain, are workaholics or televised sports addicts. But women can have intimacy issues, too. Like men, they can lose themselves in work. They can devote most of their time and energy to children and feel noble while "sacrificing" time with their intimate partners.

Intimacy in a sexual relationship cannot be sustained and nurtured without sex, which is usually the first thing to go when couples are busy, tired, and stressed.

### The Couple

Brad, thirty, and Cynthia, twenty-eight, had only been married a year when they came to see me. She had little desire for sex and seldom reached orgasm. Frustrated by her lack of interest in lovemaking, Brad put in longer and longer hours at the office. Then she got a job that took up more of her time. They didn't feel close to each other and wondered if they'd made a mistake in marrying. She accused him of being "emotionally distant," while he said she was "cold in bed."

But Brad and Cynthia, who had met while traveling with separate groups of friends in Paris, had a romantic beginning. They just had to get back to that place. Their initial Fantasy Encounter, "Rediscovering First Love" (see page 139), helped them re-create the feelings of excitement and desire that they felt for each other almost at first sight. The fantasy had a powerful effect on them. They based the week's Provocative

Encounters on acting out that and similar fantasies.

Cynthia said, "Brad put so much of himself into creating the Fantasy Encounter and Provocative Encounters that I fell in love with him all over again. Suddenly we were romantically holding hands, hugging and kissing, and behaving like honeymooners. He brought home flowers. And he came home from work earlier." He said, "I couldn't wait to get home to be with Cynthia and enjoy spending time with her. We're having fun together."

At the end of their second week in the program, they felt emotionally closer than they had been since they got married. Their most memorable Provocative Encounter from week two was a game of sexual charades. Each had to guess where and how the other wanted to be touched by body language alone—and supply that stimulation within the ten-minute time frame. Now they were ready to work toward achieving one of their sexual goals, helping Cynthia to become more orgasmic. She was able to reach orgasm via oral and manual stimulation in the Provocative Encounters, but she "wanted to make it happen" during intercourse, too.

### The Provocative Encounter: The Ultimate Orgasm Position

"Brad loves the female superior position," Cynthia said. "It was not my favorite before we started the program. I felt a little self-conscious about my body in that position. When I wasn't that interested in sex, I certainly didn't have the enthusiasm getting on top requires."

She chose the female superior position as one of their Provocative Encounters in week three. Many women find this the most advantageous intercourse position for orgasm. A woman can get the indirect clitoral stimulation she needs by controlling the angle and speed of penetration. At the same time, he or she can stroke her clitoris during intercourse. And many men, like Brad, love the position for the visual stimulation.

Cynthia bought a black bustier with satin and lace trim to wear during the Encounter. She also left on her high-heeled pumps and black thigh-high stockings. The costume made her feel "worldly and decadent" and eased her anxieties about her body. "I knew my breasts looked great," she said. "I was aroused just looking at myself in the mirror."

She and Brad stimulated one another manually until he was erect and she was well lubricated. Then she mounted him. Her goal was to bring both of them to orgasm within ten minutes—with minimal help from him. "Cynthia threw herself into intercourse like she never had," he said. "She leaned forward, tantalizing me with her breasts; and she leaned backward, stroking her clitoris as she rode me. It was one of the most arousing and satisfying lovemaking episodes of our life together."

And they both reached orgasm.

## How the Provocative Encounter Worked

They both rated the Female Superior Position Encounter as an unqualified success. The lingerie, stockings, and heels in bed were a surprise to Brad. Afterward he encouraged her to buy more lingerie. Lovemaking in costume appealed to both of them, for different reasons.

"Our real problem wasn't low desire and difficulty with orgasm," Cynthia said. "I didn't want to have sex because I didn't feel like I was a priority with Brad. The more I felt unimportant to him, the less attractive I felt. That changed in the first week of the program. As soon as he began paying attention to me, I felt sexier. Orgasms during intercourse in less than ten minutes are icing on the cake."

Brad agreed that their relationship began to improve almost immediately. Like Cynthia, he felt more desirable as a sex partner. But, he said, "her orgasms are more than icing on the cake. They're a big chunk of that cake for me. I feel like a man when she comes. I am confident that I can please my woman in bed. She isn't depressed anymore. In fact, she's genuinely happy."

"We're close again," she said. They reached their goals of greater communication and deepened intimacy. "And, we're better lovers, too."

---

## Technique: Female Superior Position

- If you're worried about your tummy or less-than-perfect breasts, wear lingerie or a partially buttoned silk shirt during intercourse. You don't have to be naked to have sex. In fact, dressing for bed can be visually stimulating and arousing for both partners.
- In the basic version of the position, he lies on his back as she straddles him and lowers herself onto his penis. He might want to put a pillow under his buttocks to raise his hips for a more efficacious angle—just as she does in the missionary position.
- She controls the angle and depth of penetration.
- Variations on the basic position include.

- Leaning back, resting her hands on the bed or floor behind her
- Leaning forward, resting her hands on the bed or floor in front of her
- Facing the opposite direction, toward his feet, allowing him a view of her buttocks
- Flattening herself out on top of him, clenching her thighs together, and rolling her clitoris into him
- Moving in a circular pattern from side to side
- Use her hands—or his—to provide additional clitoral stimulation.
- Make eye contact, especially at the point of orgasm.

*Chapter 15*

# Evaluating the Provocative Encounter

## The First Provocative Encounter Report Card

These couples all used elements of their Fantasy Encounters in their Provocative Encounters. In developing their Fantasy Encounters, they'd stated their most important sexual needs and desires—their goals—in a safe way. The Provocative Encounters helped them reach their goals by including oral sex, a specific position, fantasy role-playing, or whatever activity was central to the fantasy because it was arousing and thrilling to both partners.

### Why Do Provocative Encounters Work So Well?

- The couples use the Fantasy Encounters as mental foreplay. They design a fantasy with enough erotic appeal to keep both of them interested in it throughout the week. Instead of suppressing sexual fantasies in their daily lives as they were likely doing before the 21-Day Passion Fix program, they have learned how to nurture those fantasies. Good sex doesn't just happen.

- The prohibition against intercourse in the first week of the program gives couples a new sexual start with each other. *They can focus on sexual pleasure, not sexual performance.* If a man had performance anxieties going into the program, he can relax because he doesn't have to achieve and sustain an erection through intercourse. Both partners benefit from a kind of lovemaking that takes them back to the early days of their courtship, before they had intercourse together. They experience the joys of sexual tension all over again.

- The brief nature of the Provocative Encounters encourages creativity and experimentation. You can try almost anything for ten minutes. Trying a new activity or position in a Provocative Encounter is like tasting an unusual food.

- Provocative Encounters take sex out of a time-and-place rut. Couples don't have to limit lovemaking to the bedroom at night. They can have sex in the shower, on the kitchen floor, in the backseat of the car parked in the garage. They don't have to be undressed either.

- Because they can't do the same activity in exactly the same way during the program's nine Provocative Encounters, couples are forced to vary their lovemaking patterns. Variety is called the "spice" of sex life for a good reason.

- And, the Encounters help couples expand their definition of *sex*. Before the program, most of these couples thought "sex" had to be foreplay and intercourse. They learn they can have great sex without intercourse or without much foreplay or even without touching each other.

- Planned encounters teach couples that desire and arousal can come after sexual activity begins. They don't wait to be "in the mood." A kiss or caress ignites the passion. Waiting for spontaneous combustion can be a long wait.

- Provocative Encounters encourage couples to become better lovers. They are challenged to arouse and satisfy each other within the ten-minute time frame. To accomplish that goal, they have to develop better lovemaking techniques.

## Fine-Tuning the Provocative Encounters

How effective were your initial Provocative Encounters? Answer the following questions together to rate your own progress.

1. Did the Provocative Encounter contain elements that were arousing to each partner?
2. Did the Encounter heighten your arousal for the next sexual event?
3. Was the kissing and oral play stimulating and satisfying?
4. Was the manual play stimulating and satisfying?

5. Did you incorporate new techniques, positions, and sex toys into the Encounters?
6. Did the Encounter help you achieve your sexual goals?
7. Did you both reach orgasm? Was the experience satisfying to both of you, whether it led to orgasm or not? Was the afterplay satisfying?

PART FIVE

# PUTTING IT ALL TOGETHER

*Chapter 16*

## Week One: Provoke the Passion

COUPLES BEGIN THE 21-DAY PASSION FIX program in vastly different places. The Smiths may need an erotic jump-start to a stalled, but once satisfactory, sex life. The Joneses, on the other hand, may have to overcome problems like rapid ejaculation or difficulty with orgasm before they can enjoy lovemaking. The Smiths would be bored with the program the Joneses develop to meet their needs. And, conversely, the Joneses might give up altogether if they tried to tackle the more aggressive form of the program that works for the Smiths. They would feel pressured to perform at an uncomfortable level for them. This program works so well because every couple can follow the basic format and still create a completely individual mix of Fantasy and Provocative Encounters that is just right for them.

Now you understand why answering the questionnaire and using those answers to set your own sexual goals are such intrinsic steps to making the 21-Day Passion Fix work. Some of my clients were skeptical about the value of this process when they began. By the end of the program, however, they were believers. Those steps enabled them to create Fantasy and Provocative Encounters that were just right.

If you were sitting across from me in my office, I would help you plan your own program by matching your goals with Fantasy and Provocative Encounters for the first week. During those Encounters, you and your partner would alternate providing and receiving stimulation to cut down on performance anxiety and allow each other to luxuriate in sensual pleasure. When you came back the following week, we would talk about how the Encounters worked and use that information to develop the next week's plan—and finally, repeat the process for week three. You may not have this personal guidance in creating your own customized program, but you have an advantage none of my clients have had to date: *this book*.

As you read the stories of clients in Parts Three and Four, you likely identified with some couples more than others. Their experiences with Fantasy and Provocative Encounters should have stimulated your erotic creativity. I'm not suggesting you copy their choices exactly. But, let them be the sparks that light your fire.

## Finding Your Level

You and your partner will fall into one of three categories: high stimulation, medium stimulation, or low stimulation. These categories are labeled by the degree of erotic stimulation that is required for successful Encounters, and there is significant variation within each group. I want you to think of these categories as helpful guides, not as rigid frameworks.

An erotic massage is the first Provocative Encounter in the first week of the program for the majority of couples. Here is how that Encounter would vary according to the amount of stimulation a couple needs:

- *High stimulation:* The massage would include more focused, intense stimulation of the genitals, with a sexual goal of orgasm.
- *Medium stimulation:* The genitals would receive the same focus and intensity as the rest of the body in the massage. The goal would be to increase arousal but not necessarily include orgasm.
- *Low stimulation:* The sensual massage would not include the genitals. The sexual goal would be to diminish anxiety surrounding sexual activity and create a pleasurable experience.

In each category, the massage differs according to the individual couple's needs for sexual stimulation as well as their goals for that week. You may make so much progress toward your goals in the first week that you move into a higher category for the second or third week. Or, you may start with high-stimulation Encounters, then drop down a level to accommodate the needs of one partner who finds the pace uncomfortable.

Finding your level can help you plan Encounters that will be arousing, satisfying—and successful. Whether you choose a high-, medium-, or low-stimulation Encounter, a positive result is what counts. At the end of the chapter, I'll give you some brief suggestions for Provocative Encounters that haven't already been covered in previous chapters and show you how to adapt them depending on stimulation needed.

## The High-Stimulation Level

Sex is good, or good enough, when you have it.

Couples who enter the program at this level complain that they are "too busy," "too tired," or "too stressed" to have sex as often as they would like. When they do have sex, they are aroused and satisfied by lovemaking. Neither partner has performance problems or suffers from performance anxiety. Orgasm isn't an issue.

The rest of their relationship is basically good, too. They generally have good communication, cooperate to achieve family and personal goals, are affectionate, and enjoy each other's company. One or both, however, may say, "I don't feel as close and connected to my partner as I did."

The intimate connection will be strengthened and sustained by more frequent lovemaking.

## The Medium-Stimulation Level

Sex *was* good, but it isn't now.

One or both have complained that sex is boring, routine, stale, infrequent—or all of the above. He may have occasional problems getting or sustaining an erection. She may not reach orgasm as often as she would like. They may argue about how, as well as how often, to have sex. Variety is often an issue. He may want, for example, more oral sex, while she wants more romance and passion in their sex life.

Some of this sexual frustration has likely been translated into other areas of the relationship. Good sex smoothes the rough edges. In the absence of regular, satisfying sex, intimate partners grow more easily annoyed with each other's little imperfections.

Reviving the sexual relationship will also restore a warm and accepting intimate bond.

### The Low-Stimulation Level

Sex is disappointing and infrequent. They may not have had sex in several months, even longer. One or both partners have a performance problem. He may have erectile difficulties or rapid ejaculation. She may have difficulty reaching orgasm. They are both avoiding sex in part to avoid another "failure."

When lovemaking is rare and unsatisfying, a couple distance themselves emotionally from each other. They watch their words and monitor their actions. One or the other may say, "I feel as if I'm walking on eggshells around my partner." Or they use words to wound, increasing the distance between them. Each complains that the other is "cold," or "cruel," or "rejecting."

Couples who are this far apart need to re-establish a good sexual relationship to restore intimacy in other areas of their lives, too.

## Getting Started

Every couple, no matter what level they begin the program,

will devise an individual plan within the following basic requirements:

- They have answered the questions and set their sexual goals.
- They have agreed to commit one hour per week to the program.
- That hour includes one 30-minute Fantasy Encounter and three 10-minute Provocative Encounters. Some couples may choose not to include oral sex—cunnilingus and fellatio—in their individual programs. But all couples need to develop and improve kissing and manual techniques and learn how to arouse and satisfy each other within the 10-minute time frame.
- Finally, they will respect the prohibition against intercourse in the first week.

### Thirty-Minute Fantasy Encounter

The Fantasy Encounter has to be intense mental foreplay for *both* partners. The story you develop together can't be one person's vision and another's acquiescence. If something doesn't excite you, say, "No, that's not arousing to me. How can we change the story to make it turn me on?" But don't say, "That's disgusting" or "Why does something like that turn you on?"

And, likewise, be willing to make changes in the script without being defensive of "your" fantasy if your partner makes it clear that he or she isn't excited by its erotic content. This isn't a fight about who's going to do the laundry, run the

233

carpool, or load the dishwasher. The only way to win in this situation is cooperation: Find the common erotic ground.

Talking about sexual fantasies is initially intimidating to many couples. You may feel a little shy and awkward with each other. Feeling that way can be sexy in itself. Weren't you shy and awkward when you first became intimate? Take those feelings and use them to put you in the mood for erotic discovery.

In creating your fantasy, adapt the Fantasy Encounters in this book or borrow stories from the resources listed if writing your own erotic script is too difficult. And don't lose sight of the Fantasy Encounter's goal: intense mental foreplay. It's not enough that the Fantasy is acceptable to both partners; it must be exciting enough to sustain you throughout the week, too. When you have scripted your Fantasy Encounter to mutual satisfaction, agree that you will both fantasize this scenario during the day in advance of every Provocative Encounter that week.

### The First Provocative Encounter: A Ten-Minute Sensual/Sexual Massage

Couples who have been avoiding sex for reasons such as performance difficulties, hidden anger and resentment, or unresolved personal or relationship issues will probably choose a *sensual massage,* with no stimulation to the genitals. They need to move slowly into the program to guarantee early success. A relaxing massage without genital stimulation will enable them to give each other pleasure—with no performance expectations. That good experience will set them up for more positive Encounters.

Other couples will probably choose a *sexual massage,* including genital stimulation. They think they're too tired, too busy, or too stressed for sex. They need an arousing Encounter that will wake up their libido and have them longing for more.

You can have the massage exactly the way you want it. One partner may choose genital stimulation; the other may not. That's fine.

All Encounters should end with brief afterplay, a few minutes of mutual verbal or physical expressions of affection.

### The Second Provocative Encounter: Massage with Kissing or Oral Genital Stimulation

As always, there is a ten-minute limitation on the Encounter. The focus is on moving forward by developing or adding to the touching skills practiced in the first Encounter. Each partner adds kissing or oral stimulation to the other's genitals as part of the massage.

Couples who aren't ready for oral sex may kiss before or during the massage. Passionate kissing is an intimate expression of feeling that can be threatening for couples trying to find their way back into a sexual relationship after a long absence. They can move from a short peck on the lips to kisses on the cheeks, eyelids, throat, or other areas of the body and forego the passionate kissing until the next Encounter.

The majority of couples probably will be ready to add passionate kissing, oral genital stimulation, or both to the massage—especially if improving kissing or oral sex skills is one of their sexual goals.

## The Third Provocative Encounter: Massage with Oral or Manual Genital Stimulation

In the final Encounter of this week, add kissing and manual and oral genital stimulation to the massage. For many couples, the "massage" will be frankly sexual, with little attention paid to stroking backs, arms, and shoulders. They will be eager for a heated Encounter, probably leading to orgasm.

Other couples may devote most of the Encounter to sensual massage, with a minimal amount of kissing, and manual and oral genital stimulation. But there should be *some* genital stimulation in this Encounter. It is time to take the plunge into deeper erotic waters.

## Getting Started

Couples often say, "Getting started was the hardest part."

The 21-Day Passion Fix program challenges a lot of the standard thinking about sex therapy. It forces couples to acknowledge that some of what they believed about lovemaking falls under the category of "myth." They have to let go of those myths. For example, they have to let go of the myth that sex should be "natural and spontaneous," meaning unplanned, unexamined, and unscheduled. They will also have to let go of the myth that their partner "should just know" how to please them. Women can't expect men to know how to arouse them and bring them to orgasm without getting some guidance, and men can't hold women responsible for maintaining their erections.

The program also addresses sexual problems in a

revolutionary way by having couples do their discovery work together, placing a priority on improving sex quickly, and using fantasy as a shared form of arousal. Couples expect to be told: Schedule dates, take a romantic vacation, and devote a lot of time to making love. They may also expect to "talk about the relationship" for weeks before getting to the sex. Men are particularly pleased to hear that isn't going to happen.

Jill and David, a couple in their late thirties, found answering questions, analyzing their answers, and using those answers to develop sexual goals "a strange way to start improving" their sex life. They had to restrain themselves from "jumping ahead" to a Provocative Encounter. Laughingly, they insisted they were "too advanced for the beginners' class." Before they filled out the questionnaires, they characterized themselves as a "high-stimulation couple."

But they followed the instructions and were surprised to discover that they didn't know everything about each other after all. David said, "I didn't know she wasn't that aroused by the way I performed cunnilingus. She didn't know that I wanted more foreplay before intercourse."

Many clients have trouble getting started because they are reluctant to schedule Encounters. "We won't be able to make love by appointment," said Cathy, forty-eight. Her husband, Mel, fifty-five, worried about being able "to perform on demand." He said, "Everything has to be perfect for us to have sex. That can't happen three times in one week." A couple who considered themselves at the medium-stimulation level, Mel and Cathy had trouble believing that each could become aroused, and frequently satisfied, within the ten-minute time frame. But, they could.

Other couples, particularly the women, have difficulty accepting that a brief encounter could possibly be better than a long one. Kerry and Todd, in their late twenties, wanted to combine the Fantasy Encounter and all three Provocative Encounters into an hour of lovemaking per week. "I hate Quickies," Kerry protested. "They're just for men." At the low-stimulation level when they began the program, Kerry and Todd moved into the high-stimulation level by week three because Kerry found the Provocative Encounters so exciting. She had her first "under an hour" orgasm in the first Encounter of week two.

No matter what your initial reservations are, you have to follow the program because:

- The Fantasy Encounter creates and sustains sexual tension throughout the week.
- Provocative Encounters increase arousal and sexual tension more effectively than longer episodes of love-making do.
- Scheduled sex will happen if you both commit to the schedule; spontaneous sex may not.
- Planning creates sexual anticipation, which leads to sexual arousal in a shorter period. (Engaging in sexual behavior, even in the absence of desire, stimulates erotic interest that will build into desire and arousal.)
- You must have immediate positive results to improve your sex life.

## *What to Expect from Week One*

Many couples will experience some difficulty in starting the 21-Day Passion Fix program. Whenever you begin a course of study, an exercise program, or any other new endeavor, you can expect to encounter a rough spot or two. But, if you do the necessary groundwork to define your sexual goals and plan Encounters that will help you reach those goals, you'll overcome the obstacles and achieve at least some success immediately.

Most couples are thrilled with the progress they make in the first week alone. By the end of that week, you and your partner can expect to increase desire and arousal, elevate the level of sexual tension between you, and improve your manual and oral lovemaking skills, including kissing. You will be thinking about sex more often, and in more positive ways, and be feeling more sensual, sexual, and alive.

### *If You Are Having Trouble Getting Started . . . Just Do It.*

Even if you don't believe it will work, give the program a chance by following the key precepts. Remember why you bought this book in the first place. You or your partner is dissatisfied with the sexual relationship. And, if one partner is dissatisfied, there is a problem. The other can't say, "It works for me." If it doesn't work for both of you, it doesn't work.

Push yourself past your anxiety. Start talking to each other about your needs, desires, fears, and sexual concerns. That's a lot more productive than saying, "Oh, this can't work for us" and retreating under the cover of your anxiety blanket.

You will change those negative attitudes about your sexual relationship when you see immediate, positive results in week one. And, you will.

### Talking about Sex

For some couples, talking about sex is difficult. They may communicate well in general, but not when the subject is sex. Or they may have difficulty talking about other important issues, too. If a man and woman can't talk about money, religion, politics, or their families, they won't find sex an easy subject.

"I'm afraid I'll hurt my partner's feelings" is a frequent justification for not opening up sexually. That was the excuse Sharon, twenty-six, used for not telling her husband, Randy, thirty-six, that she'd never had an orgasm with him. "I was afraid he'd feel threatened," she said after she'd "spilled all her secrets" in the answers to the questionnaire. He didn't feel threatened.

"I felt challenged to give her an orgasm," Randy said, "but I also told her that I really believe it's up to her to make sure she gets one."

Sharon's honest answers opened a dialogue between them and helped them develop Encounters that blended his high-stimulation desires for more oral sex with her low-stimulation needs for more affection and caressing. Fortunately they were able to talk about their sexual issues without anger. Some couples have repressed their sexual feelings for so long that they don't know how to talk without anger and frustration.

Jenny, forty-one, and Bob, forty-six, almost abandoned the program at the start because they couldn't talk about establishing sexual goals without "screaming insults" at each other. She said, "We each blamed the other for not being an exciting lover. I went into the first Provocative Encounter with the attitude, 'This can't work,' but I actually felt my anger ebb away as he massaged my body. It was magic."

And some couples have trouble talking about sex because one or both fear rejection. "If I tell my partner what I want, he [or she] will be offended" is a common excuse for keeping silent. Marty and Karen, in their mid-fifties, had never really shared their sexual desires in almost twenty years of marriage. Karen longed for him to be a more dominant lover. Marty felt "stifled" by the lack of creativity in their sex life. Neither thought the other could "take hearing" the truth. Each really feared being rejected for having such specific erotic needs.

For all these couples and others like them, talking allayed their fears. They discovered their partners were more accepting than they had imagined possible. And, as one client said, "All that talking about sex really got us aroused. We hadn't talked dirty to one another in ten years. We'd forgotten how titillating it is."

### If You Are Having Trouble Talking about Sex

Start with something easy. For example, tell him how good his caresses or kisses make you feel. Or tell her you find her attractive and sexy. You don't have to begin the conversation with a list of demands.

Practice discretion, diplomacy, and tact. You don't have to wound your partner when you suggest ways of changing and improving lovemaking. Honesty doesn't require saying, "Your body was more arousing twenty years ago." You want your partner to hear what you have to say, not shut down to avoid being hurt.

Don't attack and blame. It isn't his fault she has low desire or her fault that he does. Assigning blame puts you on opposing sides. It's hard to have good sex across a wide divide.

Be constructive, warm, and positive in your suggestions for change. Say, "Honey, I love having sex with you. I feel so much closer to you after we make love. Can we have making love more often as one of our sexual goals?"

## Creating Fantasies

Sharing sexual fantasies is intimidating for many couples. When they first hear about the Fantasy Encounter, some of my clients leap to the conclusion that they have to share their own fantasies with their partners. This is, in fact, one of the biggest misconceptions couples have about the 21-Day Passion Fix Program. In my program, *Fantasy* has a much larger and more creative definition.

The Fantasy Encounter is an erotic fairy tale created by the couple. They share their vision of a sexual "happily ever after." That fairy tale can begin in the story of their initial attraction. It can be set in a romantic, even imaginary, locale, in a time past, present, or future.

They do *not* have to confess that they sometimes fantasize making love to their husband's brother or their wife's best friend or they have had the occasional violent fantasy. I would rather they didn't! Those fantasies are best kept secret in most marriages.

Greg, fifty-eight, said, "I could never share my fantasies with Natalie. She would find them offensive." And Natalie said, "I don't want to know what goes on in his mind about sex. Once I looked over his shoulder while he was online. He was looking at some disgusting pictures. If that's his fantasy, I don't want to share it."

Her fantasies, Natalie said, were romantic and soft. Greg and Natalie seemed to be far apart in this and other sexual areas. At first, they said they couldn't remember their early feelings of attraction. I told them not to share their secret fantasies or worry that they couldn't remember that attraction, but to develop a new story. If they could fantasize being romantic erotic characters, who would they be? They used a variation of the conquering hero and the virginal maiden as their initial Fantasy Encounter. Both found it arousing.

Developing a successful Fantasy motivates a couple to get started in the program. They feel more connected to each other. And they also experience themselves as more sensual and sexual individuals. Getting couples in touch with their own ability to fantasize is one of the program's great strengths.

## If You Are Having Trouble Creating Fantasies . . .

Go back to the beginning and recall every erotic detail of those early days together.

I encourage couples to begin developing their Fantasy Encounter by sharing their remembered sexual and romantic feelings of their initial attraction. Then I ask them to take that attraction and move it to an exotic place far from their daily lives. They fantasize themselves meeting in this setting, whether it's Paris, Bombay, or an island in the South Pacific, and sharing the same intense feelings they did in real life. Many couples successfully use a variation of "Sex on the Beach" (see page 82) as their initial Fantasy Encounter.

Maybe you can't go back there. Some couples feel too alienated to recall their strong initial attraction. Maybe they never had one; perhaps they married for other reasons such as security. And some couples feel awkward or even sad going back to the memory of their early days together. They dwell on unfulfilled promises or passion gone cold. Others simply have difficulty expressing the feelings their memories generate.

For these couples, I suggest reading aloud to each other from the fantasies in this book or from other resources. Become actors. Find romantic and sexual characters and role-play them. Develop a script that works for these two exciting leads.

Don't be critical or judgmental of each other's contributions. You can say, "That doesn't excite me," but don't say, "Oh, that's weird." A good suggestion if you feel awkward in developing a Fantasy Encounter is to start with a milder, less threatening fantasy. And then later, you can spice it up in subsequent weeks, when you feel more daring.

## Integrating Goals

Frequently one partner wants to move more aggressively through the program than the other does. She wants high-stimulation Encounters, while he needs a slower pace. This is a familiar situation for them, because the high-stimulation partner is likely the one who has wanted more frequent love-making, more sexual variety, and different positions or practices, all of which the other rejects.

Merry, thirty-five, and Rick, thirty-one, initially saw the program as an opportunity for forcing the other to take sex at her or his pace. "She rarely performs oral sex," he said. "She doesn't want to have sex very often. When we do, it's sex in the same old way. I am bored and frustrated with our sex life." She countered by saying his demands were "excessive."

I was able to convince Rick and Merry that their success in the program depended on their ability to cooperate in meshing their needs and desires into goals they could both comfortably pursue. Rick had to be patient and willing to work harder at pleasing Merry than vice versa. Merry had to push herself to do things that made her feel anxious and uncomfortable. The first week moved at her pace, with low-stimulation Encounters such as the sensual body massage with no genital or breast stimulation. By the second week, Merry was ready to move into medium-stimulation Encounters, with oral sex for both of them (a shorter time for cunnilingus) combined with body massage. They planned high-stimulation Encounters in the third week, including more advanced oral techniques, with orgasm as a goal for her, and vigorous Quickie intercourse positions. Romantic ambiance—including candles, incense, and soft lighting—was a part of every Encounter. They met all their goals, including more frequent and varied lovemaking.

Often one partner is more motivated to make the 21-Day Passion Fix program work. Typically that partner is the more dissatisfied of the two. He or she wants change, while the other may be clinging to the status quo, out of fear if for no other reason. I encourage the more highly motivated partner to make the first concessions in developing Fantasy and

Provocative Encounters. But that doesn't mean he or she "gives in" to the partner's demands.

### If You Are Having Difficulty Integrating Goals . . .

Negotiating differences in developing goals can arouse buried anger and resentment. These emotions didn't just develop; they've been under the surface for a long time. If you are feeling angry, frustrated, and impatient with your partner who doesn't want to move at your pace, don't repress the feelings. Talk about them, without being cruel and casting blame. It will be easier to move ahead once you've gotten past this.

Shelve all your old excuses for not having sex more often or in more exciting ways. "I'm not in the mood" doesn't fly anymore. Don't wait to feel motivated. Just get started.

Don't view erotic compromise as not getting everything you want. You can't turn the process of setting goals into a contest of wills. If you do that, you both lose.

## Overcoming Inhibitions and Performance Problems

The couples who generally have the most difficulty in the first week of the program are those with chronic low desire, deep-seated inhibitions, or performance issues and problems, including poor lovemaking skills. As soon as they achieve some success, these couples become more motivated. Taking the first step to overcome their emotional obstacles, however, can feel like beginning a climb up Everest.

Christine and Miguel, in their mid-thirties, married as teenagers because she was pregnant. "We never had a good sex life," he said. Both had performance problems. He suffered from rapid ejaculation, which he blamed on her desire for him to "just get it over" when they made love. Christine rarely reached orgasm and had chronic low desire. "And she doesn't even want to talk about sex," Miguel said. "She's very inhibited about sex. I can't get her to tell me what she likes." They were going to get a divorce but decided "for the sake of the children" to give their marriage one last effort.

If that effort had required more than one hour per week for three weeks, Christine and Miguel probably would not have made it. They were too tired and discouraged for anything more. They began with low-stimulation Encounters, focused on non-genital body massage and then outercourse, kissing, caressing, and massaging each other's bodies while clothed. They rediscovered the desire they felt as teenagers, before Christine got pregnant. They were able to focus on the erotic moments of their early days together, not the traumatic ones. And they built on the desire that had been short-circuited in real life. By the end of the third week, Christine was able to reach orgasm during lovemaking.

Their story, while dramatic, isn't unusual in this program. When couples with sexual problems are able to focus solely on feeling sensual and sexual for brief periods, they begin to overcome their inhibitions and performance problems. With simple, easy-to-follow directions, they learn how to become good lovers in a situation where expectations are low and chances for success are high.

If they can do it, so can you and your partner.

### If You Are Having Difficulty Overcoming Inhibitions and Performance Problems . . .

At the risk of sounding repetitious: Get started.

You have to ignore your fears, anxieties, and skepticism about the program and plunge ahead. People generally begin doing better as soon as they make an effort to change. You have to create desire, not wait for it to happen. Act as if you have desire and you will.

If you're worried about disappointing your partner because your lovemaking skills aren't proficient, put that out of your mind. He or she will be pleased that you're trying. Remember that lovemaking is a joint venture. You aren't solely responsible for making it good.

Practice helps improve sexual techniques. Even awkward lovers show progress quickly. They start acquiring sexual skills in the first week because the brevity of the ten-minute Encounter gives them the courage to try new things. Follow the directions for the positions and practices in the proceeding chapters—and surprise yourself at how well you can make love.

## Measuring Your Progress Toward Your Goals

At the end of every week, make time to sit down together and answer these seven questions. Use your answers to help determine how much progress you've made toward achieving your sexual goals. This information will help you plan the next week's Encounters.

1. Did the Fantasy Encounter increase sexual tension and desire?
2. Did the Provocative Encounters heighten your sexual arousal?
3. Was the massage part of the Provocative Encounters sensual and arousing?
4. Did the kissing create feelings of desire and increased intimacy?
5. Was the manual stimulation arousing?
6. Was the oral sex arousing?
7. Did you have an orgasm? Was the afterplay satisfying?

## Some Provocative Encounter Suggestions for Week One

You can vary a Provocative Encounter to meet high-, medium-, or low-stimulation needs. Take a look at the ones already described or those suggested in this section. In general, a low-stimulation Encounter in the first week will have minimal genital contact (or none) and orgasm will not be a goal. Genital stimulation increases in a medium-stimulation Encounter, and orgasm may or may not be a goal. For a high-stimulation Encounter, genital stimulation is focused and intense, with orgasm a goal.

**Role-Playing.** Use your own Fantasy Encounter or one of the others in this book. Act out the roles with sexual contact.

**Sex in the Shower.** Taking an erotic shower together is a thrill. Soapsuds can replace the oil or lotion you would use in a sensual massage. Rub each other's bodies. Kiss under the cascading water. And use water jets to provide mutual genital stimulation.

**The Car Wash Cuddle.** Kiss, caress, and fondle each other while taking the car through the car wash. This is an excellent opportunity to practice mutual manual genital stimulation. Sitting side by side encourages different hand positions than you would be using in bed.

**The Morning Wake-Up Call.** Set the alarm for ten minutes earlier than normal. Wake him or her by sliding under the covers and performing manual stimulation and/or oral sex.

**The Midnight Moment.** Set your alarm clock to wake you up three or four hours after bedtime. Caress, cuddle, and stimulate each other's genitals for ten minutes; then, go back to sleep. You'll wake up filled with desire.

*Chapter 17*

# Week Two: Practice the Passion

THE COUPLES IN MY PRACTICE are typically more optimistic about the program at the start of week two than they were the week before. As long as they've had realistic expectations, they've made progress toward their sexual goals. That progress has increased their confidence in their ability to change their sex lives. They are generally enthusiastic about planning the Fantasy and Provocative Encounters—and they expect positive results.

I hope that you and your partner are starting the week in a good place, too. Before you write the script for your second Fantasy Encounter, however, take ten or fifteen minutes to look back at your sexual goals, estimate your progress toward achieving them, and decide together what you want to accomplish this week. You may need to create Provocative Encounters with more, or less, stimulation than last week. Your goals may seem too modest or too ambitious.

Now that you know what to expect in the 21-Day Passion Fix program, you can make it work even better for you in week two.

## *Review and Re-evaluate Your Sexual Goals*

If you haven't met your sexual goals from week one, re-evaluate those goals. Did the Fantasy and Provocative Encounters help you make progress toward them? The answer may be "Yes, some, but not enough." Why not? What didn't work?

The problems you identify will likely fall into one of the following categories:

1. *The goals were unrealistic.* A woman who has avoided oral sex for a decade, for example, probably won't be successful at a Provocative Encounter based on fellatio. A couple who has been angry at each other for months or years aren't likely to become playful and passionate immediately. A Fantasy Encounter that casts them in the roles of playful lovers probably won't be as effective as they need it to be. In setting goals, a couple has to take their sexual past and each partner's fears and inhibitions into consideration.

Kerry and Martin, in their late thirties, were disappointed in their first week's progress. "One of our goals was to make Kerry become aroused more quickly," he said. "I focused a lot of manual and oral attention on her during the Provocative Encounters, but she didn't reach orgasm."

"I did get very aroused," Kerry said. "And I might have reached orgasm if you hadn't been 'focusing' as hard as you were. I felt like a science experiment."

In the second week, Martin used a lighter touch in Encounters that also permitted some eye contact, building the kind of intimacy Kerry needed in order to feel as though she was being loved and not treated as the goal itself. They agreed that her orgasm wouldn't be an obsessive goal. As soon as they relaxed, of course, Kerry had an orgasm during a Provocative Encounter.

2. *One partner didn't have much input in setting goals.* He or she may have been reluctant to participate in the program, forcing the other to take charge. That dynamic works for some couples, because the reluctant partner is able to enjoy the Encounters anyway. But sometimes the uninvolved partner holds back emotionally and plays the role of critical observer. "I didn't want to do this anyway" is the fallback position.

Occasionally one partner is too shy or inhibited to play an active role in setting goals and developing Encounters. Again, that can work for a couple if the shy partner agrees to participate as actively as possible in the Encounters. Receiving pleasure can make a partner feel desired enough to overcome shyness and inhibitions.

June, forty-three, and her husband, Rob, fifty-four, considered giving up on the program after the first week because she refused to help plan the Encounters but still criticized his choices. "I can't please her," Rob said, "sexually or otherwise." When he said he was ready to give up on her, not just on the program, June broke down in tears and admitted that she was afraid she couldn't meet the high erotic expectations Rob had listed as his goals.

"He's much more experienced than I am," June said. "I am scared of failure."

Once he understood her fears, Rob adjusted his goals. They worked together on planning the second week's events. And, not surprisingly, they had a great deal more success.

3. *The partners weren't entirely honest with each other when they identified their sexual goals.* One or both may have withheld information, fearing their partner would find the truth uncomfortable, not arousing, or hurtful. A woman, for example, might be embarrassed to admit her desire to be dominated by her partner. He might not want to tell her that he isn't excited by the way she touches his penis. They may not have answered the questionnaire truthfully either. Honesty is crucial to setting realistic goals.

Jennifer, twenty-nine, and Josh, twenty-eight, shaded the truth considerably when they answered the questionnaire. "I didn't want him to know that I'd never had an orgasm during intercourse," Jennifer said. "I didn't know how to tell her that she has habits that annoy me in bed," Josh admitted, "like sucking my nipples and putting her finger in my anus."

They went back to the questionnaires, corrected their misleading answers, and re-evaluated their goals. "Just doing that made the Encounters work better for us in the second week," Jennifer said. "We didn't have guilt over telling each other lies." They also knew that Jennifer wasn't going to have her first orgasm during intercourse unless Josh also provided the kind of manual stimulation he gave her during "foreplay."

4. *The partner wanting to move more aggressively into the program may have taken the upper hand in setting the goals.* Sometimes couples try to accomplish more than they reasonably can in the first week, especially if one of them is determined to set a fast pace. They create high-stimulation Encounters that leave them feeling more anxious than aroused. Like an out-of-shape couple who tries to begin an exercise program on high speed,

they set themselves up for "failures" and disappointments.

Tim, fifty-eight, and Gabrielle, fifty-three, wanted to "make up for lost time." She said, "Once we decided to turn our sex life around, we wanted to do it right away. If *any* couple could do that in three weeks, we wanted to achieve *our* goals in one."

Though Tim had problems with erectile dysfunction and Gabrielle had inhibitions about oral sex, they expected to resolve all their issues and problems in seven days. When Tim had trouble with sustaining arousal and Gabrielle repeatedly gagged while attempting to perform ten minutes of fellatio in their second Provocative Encounter, they were discouraged. Fortunately they knew what to do at the start of week two: Take it slower and focus on building their skills. "We finally did make up for lost time," Tim reported.

## Better Planning

If you didn't make real progress last week, you can still move ahead this week. Better planning is the key. But how can you plan this week's events so they will be more arousing and satisfying for both partners?

- Select the positive experiences from the first week's Encounters. Was his genital massage exciting? Did she hold his penis in the way he's always wanted it held?
- Build on those experiences in developing the second week's Encounters.
- If something didn't work, modify it—a low-stimulation

Provocative Encounter, for example, that includes more kissing and caressing, and less oral sex.

- Be realistic about goals. And don't judge yourself or your partner harshly.

I define a successful week in broad terms. You've succeeded if you made some progress toward achieving your goals. Changes in attitudes are as significant as changes in behavior. A woman who has shown willingness to overcome her inhibitions and allow her husband to stimulate her manually and orally has come as far as another woman, more comfortable with these practices, who has an orgasm via cunnilingus. A man who's been suffering from chronic impotence but tries to accommodate his partner's sexual needs in spite of his anxiety has shown his willingness to push through inhibitions, performance anxieties, and other personal fears.

As long as both partners participate in the Fantasy Encounters and three Provocative Encounters each week of the program, they have met their basic goals.

## *Moving Forward*

In week two, you and your partner will expand and improve the manual and oral techniques you learned last week. Your Encounters will place a greater emphasis on skill development. And you'll add sex toys and Quickie intercourse positions to the Provocative Encounters.

## Fantasy Encounter

Sometimes couples want to repeat or just slightly revise their initial Fantasy for week two because they found it so stimulating. Don't give in to that temptation. You need to create a new script. Last week's Fantasy will lose some of its ability to arouse if you use it again.

And your Fantasy Encounter should include specific love-making skills that you talk about in graphic detail. In the initial Fantasy Encounter, you may have fantasized about him ravishing her. Well, in this Encounter, add the juicy details. Where and how will you touch, kiss, caress, and fondle each other?

## Provocative Encounters

All three Provocative Encounters, each at least ten minutes long, should include kissing and manual and oral stimulation. At least two of the three Encounters must also include the use of a sex toy and a Quickie intercourse position. And no repeats! Two different sex toys, two different intercourse positions. You can't find a comfortable new position and keep using it. Isn't that partly how you got where you were at the beginning of last week?

But you can start with "easy" positions, saving the more physically demanding or complicated positions for week three. If you have low-stimulation needs, begin using sex toys only briefly, even on areas other than the genitals in your first Encounters with them. Strap a vibrator on the back of your hand, for example, and massage shoulders, arms, legs, and thighs.

The goal is to move forward, but you don't have to take big steps every day. Some couples need to introduce innovations in small doses to make the program work for them. They move in small steps toward their goals. And that's okay. Move forward at your own pace. It's the direction, not the speed that counts.

## What to Expect from Week Two

Desire and arousal will continue to increase. Women will find they are reaching orgasm more quickly now than they did during lovemaking in the past. Men will gain greater control over their erections and ejaculations. Couples who came into the program with low desire may have pushed themselves to participate in the first week's Encounters. Now they're looking forward to them. They begin the second week with higher levels of desire, confident that they will find the Encounters arousing and pleasurable.

Couples with performance problems or orgasm difficulties probably enter the second week with some anxiety. The prohibition against intercourse in the first week enabled men with erectile problems to relax and concentrate on giving and receiving sensual and sexual stimulation. Now they are faced with performance issues again. How can a man participate in a Provocative Encounter based on a Quickie position if he isn't sure he'll be able to maintain an erection?

And what about her? As the emphasis shifts to intercourse, she worries that her orgasm will become an issue again. She fears the pressure is on her to become orgasmic quickly. "Now

I know I have to reach orgasm or be a failure in the program, because making me orgasmic is one of our goals," a client said.

But that is a distortion of the goal-setting process. One of his goals might be improving the quality of his erections or sustaining them during lovemaking. One of her goals might be becoming more orgasmic during intercourse. That doesn't mean they are failures if he doesn't have a strong erection throughout the Encounter or she doesn't reach orgasm at the end of it. Any *attempt* toward achieving goals can be counted as a success.

Regardless of what level you were at sexually when you entered the program, you and your partner will feel more attractive in general, and to each other in particular, by the end of this week. The emotional connection will continue to intensify. You will become more sensual. And you'll make progress toward your sexual goals, maybe in small steps, maybe in larger ones. Many couples tell me they feel "more alive" after two weeks in the program than they've felt in years, sometimes decades, because the Fantasy and Provocative Encounters have taught them how to stimulate their own, as well as their partner's, sensuality.

A sexual experience actually begins in your head long before the Provocative Encounter.

## Graphic Sexual Communication

In week two, the Provocative Encounters focus more specifically on the sexual skills necessary for arousing and satisfying each other. Some couples have trouble telling each other what they want in graphic language. "I don't know how to tell him how to lick me," a client said, blushing in front of her husband of twenty years. One or both partners may also have trouble hearing what the other has to say. He may hear her suggestions for giving her oral and manual stimulation as a criticism of the way he makes love. She may experience his directions as demands. As one client put it, "Sexual communication jumps up a level in week two."

Cassie and Mark, in their early thirties, found "giving each other sex directions" the most difficult part of the program. "When I told him how I wanted to be kissed, he got defensive," Cassie said. "I asked him to kiss one lip at a time gently, and then kiss both lips for a minute before putting the tip of his tongue in my mouth. He got mad. And, he accused me of faking all the kisses we'd shared in the past."

When Cassie asked Mark to tell her how to do something in a different way than she usually did, he felt less threatened by her "instructions." He told her that he wanted her to lick and suck his testicles, even try to hold them in her mouth, as part of fellatio. Cassie was happy to oblige. Her enthusiastic cooperation enabled Mark to relax and let her tell him what she wanted too.

### If You Are Having Trouble with Graphic Sexual Communication . . .

Choose your words carefully. "I would like to try that position this way" is better than "I don't like the way you've been doing it." Try to ask for what you want in a breathless, excited way that indicates your desire. Whatever tone of voice you choose, don't be cool and clinical.

Show, rather than tell, your partner what you want

whenever you can. Good, constructive dialogue about technique includes a lot of illustration. Put your hand on your own body. Guide his or her hand with yours.

Read from this book and other sources. Use videos. Pause the action at the arousing part. Together you can analyze how to make that move.

Let go of the past. Don't resurrect the old arguments about what he or she does "wrong" in bed.

### Sex Toys

Some of my clients have reacted with surprise, even dismay, to the idea of incorporating sex toys into their love-making. "It's unnatural," said one woman who rarely reached orgasm—until her husband used a vibrator on her. "Electronic gadgets will make sex feel less intimate," protested a man who hadn't been sexually intimate with his wife in three months when they came to see me. Their responses are not uncommon. People who couldn't function without their cell phones, pagers, PalmPilots, and other electronic accoutrements suddenly become naturalists when the subject is sex.

The "natural" way of making love, they argue, is one naked couple under the sheets in a darkened bedroom. No wonder they're bored with their sex lives. Vibrators and other toys, flavored lotions and oils, adult videos, ribbed condoms, and even edible panties are novelty items for enhancing sex. Using them makes sex different, often more exciting, and definitely fun. Too many couples have forgotten, or never learned, how to play sexually.

"We should be able to turn each other on without using

these props," insisted Grace, forty-two. Her younger husband, Tom, thirty-two, was more willing "to give technology a try." Still, Grace held out. "I'll do everything except the sex toys," she said. Finally, she reached a compromise with her husband: Tom could use a small palm-size vibrator on every part of her body except her genitals. Grace loved the sensations. After the first session, she was willing to let him use that vibrator everywhere.

Other couples rebel at the mention of sex toys because "they're tacky." Matt and Barbara, in their early fifties, considered sex toys and adult videos "products for horny young men, lonely older singles, or trailer park couples." But they hadn't watched a video or looked through a sex toy catalogue in a decade. The products have improved immensely in that time. The erotic marketplace is filled with variety, including many quality items marketed for couples. While Matt and Barbara were dubious, they agreed to look for suitable toys and videos—and had no trouble finding them. Barbara selected an Eastern arts lovemaking kit that included oils, candles, directions for intercourse positions, incense, honey dust (meant for licking), and a small vibrator on a belt to stimulate both partners during intercourse.

Sex therapists and medical doctors have played an advisory role in designing many of the products marketed today. Some therapists have produced videos. And women, like Candida Royalle, successfully market lines of videos aimed at couples, not guys at stag parties. Many videos are educational as well as arousing.

A modern sex life without adult toys and videos is like television in the days before cable, VCRs, and DVD players.

## If You Are Still Not Comfortable Using Sex Toys . . .

Start small. Buy a package of ribbed, colored, flavored, or otherwise unusual condoms and play with them, especially if you haven't used condoms in years. Try a small vibrator first. Save the giant-size model with multiple attachments for next week.

Buy a sensual lovemaking kit containing oils, lotions, and other nonthreatening products. Look for one containing honey dust. It really is made from honey—and can be licked off everywhere.

Rent a mainstream movie with erotic content, like *The English Patient* or *Eyes Wide Shut,* rather than an X-rated movie. French and Italian films are wonderful. Read the boxes for inspiration. Buy a video guide that lists and rates films in "sexy" or "erotic" categories. (And see my list on page 153.)

### Quickie Positions

Accepting the concept that brief, intense sexual encounters can dramatically improve their sex life is difficult for many couples. It challenges them to re-examine their attitudes and beliefs about lovemaking. They have been taught to believe, for example, that long lovemaking sessions are superior to brief encounters, especially from the woman's perspective. Even men, who are generally more predisposed to find the Quickie appealing, have trouble believing that it is the path to better sex.

In week one, the Provocative Encounters seemed more like foreplay than Quickies because intercourse was prohibited.

Now in the second week, couples must include intercourse in their Encounters. And intercourse in ten minutes sounds intimidating. They are worried that she won't be sufficiently aroused or satisfied.

Charles and Megan, both nearly forty, were sure their Encounters "would inevitably fail" because she had never been satisfied when lovemaking lasted less than thirty minutes. "Megan will just be getting started when it's over," Charles said. "She gets tense when we make love and she doesn't finish," meaning reach orgasm.

They had to redefine *sex,* because their "no-hands" version of intercourse took so much time that they rarely made love. Charles was able to sustain an erection by stopping intercourse and moving to other kinds of lovemaking until Megan was sufficiently aroused by the kissing, caressing, and oral sex that she was finally able to reach orgasm via intercourse alone. Like many couples, Charles and Megan thought her orgasm had to precede his, because ejaculation signaled the end. Well, it doesn't. A man can continue stimulating his partner manually after his ejaculation. Or she can stimulate herself.

Charles and Megan were surprised to discover that she could become aroused and satisfied in ten minutes—when the Encounters included manual stimulation during intercourse. "We also used positions that gave her more friction against her clitoris," Charles said. "We experimented with different positions more in one week than we had in the previous decade."

Some couples find the Quickie intercourse positions awkward at first. They are accustomed to making love in bed in one of two standard positions: the man-on-top, known as the "missionary" position, or the woman-on-top, the female superior position. There's nothing wrong with these positions. But couples need to use more positions—and to adapt the basic two to make them more creative and interesting.

Provocative Encounters do work. A brief encounter can fit into any schedule. Long lovemaking sessions can't. The intercourse positions in Provocative Encounters aren't old-fashioned Quickies. They require skill and sensitivity to the partner's needs and desires. Even if you don't fully believe in the concept, try it.

You'll be surprised—and thrilled—with the results.

### If You Are Having Difficulty with Quickies . . .

A suggested position may not work for you and your partner when you follow the directions in this book or another resource. Adapt it and try again. Still doesn't work? Move on. Try something else. There are dozens of intercourse positions.

Don't get discouraged because a position that sounds hot when another couple describes it doesn't create fireworks for you and your partner. Every couple is a unique combination of two bodies.

Remember that each attempt at a new position is a learning experience. You learn something about each other's bodies and responses whether the position works well or it doesn't. The more new positions and practices you try, the more you learn.

And the more you experiment, the less inhibited and more creative you will be together sexually. That erotic courage increases your odds of successful lovemaking. Even men who have lost confidence in their ability to sustain an erection can find positions that help them "perform."

## Measuring Your Progress Toward Your Goals

Answer these seven questions together to evaluate your progress. Use your answers to help plan next week's Fantasy and Provocative Encounters.

1. Did the Fantasy Encounter increase tension and desire more quickly this week than last?
2. Did the Provocative Encounters heighten your sexual arousal more this week than last?
3. Was the manual stimulation more arousing?
4. Was the kissing and/or oral stimulation more arousing?
5. Did the use of sex toys heighten desire and arousal?
6. Did the Quickie intercourse positions heighten intimacy and arousal?
7. Were you and your partner orgasmic? Was the afterplay more satisfying?

## Some Quickie Position Suggestions for Week Two

In addition to the positions already suggested, you may want to try the following ideas. Also, you will find directions for many other variations in the books I've recommended on page 151. A high-stimulation provocative encounter in week two differs from a medium- or low-stimulation one in how creative your choice is and how ambitious you are in the pursuit of your sexual goals.

**Side of the Bed, or Love Seat, Position.** This position is especially good for men with erectile difficulties because his body is elevated in an angle encouraging penetration, even with a semierect penis. A time bonus: You don't have to get undressed. He leans against the side of the bed or love seat facing his partner who is kneeling on the bed. Facing him, she lowers herself onto him so that he can enter her in a semistanding position.

**Sex on the Washing Machine.** If he isn't tall enough to do this position comfortably—and most men aren't—he can stand on something sturdy to reach the right height. She sits on top of the washing machine during the spin cycle. He enters her and has intercourse from a standing position.

A popular alternative: She sits on the dryer while he performs cunnilingus or manually stimulates her. This is an exciting position for him as well as her because he has good access tactilely as well as visually to her vagina.

**The X, or Scissors, Position.** Imagine your bodies in a sitting sex position are forming an X, with the connection at the genitals. The man sits at the edge of the bed facing the footboard with his back straight and one leg outstretched on the bed; the other leg is outstretched toward the floor or braced up on a straight-back chair placed by the bed. Her back supported against a pile of firm pillows, the woman sits astride her partner, with both legs braced on his shoulders.

It sounds awkward at first, but it's very comfortable—even for couples who aren't in prime physical shape.

## Chapter 18

# *Week Three: Intensify the Passion*

MOST COUPLES IN MY PRACTICE approach week three with confidence and enthusiasm because they have achieved success in the program. They've changed some of their attitudes about sex as well as their behavior. Now they are beginning to see themselves as creative lovers, capable of sustaining a passionate connection. They are better able to arouse and satisfy each other. Their sex lives are more exciting and orgasmic. They are making love more often, a goal of nearly everyone who has come into my office since I began practicing. And they finally realize that "no time" is no excuse for not having sex.

In the third week, most couples can put it all together. They have learned new oral and manual lovemaking skills. They have been using sex toys; for some couples, this is a new and different experience. They've tried new intercourse positions. If they had performance problems or other issues, they have made progress toward resolving them. Now they are ready to have the most exciting and innovative sex they've ever had.

But, some couples, specifically those who entered the program with performance and orgasm problems, may feel as though they're just beginning to make progress by the end of week three. The first week and maybe part of the second were devoted to making each other comfortable with sensual and sexual expression. For them, repeating the entire 21-Day Passion Fix program or repeating one or two weeks will also give them the opportunity to pull everything together.

## Turning Up the Heat

In week three, you and your partner will have more intense Fantasy and Provocative Encounters. You'll continue to expand and improve the manual and oral techniques you've learned. And you'll be more creative in using sex toys and adapting intercourse positions.

### Fantasy Encounter

Make this Fantasy Encounter as imaginative and thrilling as you can. By now, you and your partner are skilled at using fantasy to create desire and stimulate arousal in advance of Provocative Encounters. You can talk more easily about sexual scenarios and exchange ideas without fear of being ridiculed or rejected. Two weeks ago, you may have been too shy or guarded to suggest certain sexual practices, even in fantasy. Now you are bolder.

Design this Fantasy Encounter around erotic situations that seemed too threatening when you began the program.

You might, for example, explore themes of dominance and submission, anal sex, making love in public places, or other "taboos." At this point in the program, fantasy exploration should feel safe to you and your partner because neither of you feels compelled to act out these fantasies. You both understand that the power of the Fantasy is mental, not physical enactment. Let your erotic minds run wild.

### *Provocative Encounters*

As in week two, all three Provocative Encounters, each at least ten minutes long, must include kissing and manual and oral stimulation. All three Encounters should also include a Quickie intercourse position and the use of one sex toy. Again, no repeat events. That proviso encourages you and your partner to be imaginative in sex toy play and in devising variations on intercourse positions.

This week try some of the more challenging Quickie positions. Remember: You can do anything for ten minutes. If you don't like a position, you never have to do it again.

And this week incorporate your Provocative Encounters into those real-life "opportunities" that you didn't consider as "time for sex" in the past. For example, schedule a Quickie in the ten minutes before you have to leave the house to make the train for work or attend a dinner party. Plan sex in the laundry room while you're doing the week's laundry, in the kitchen while you're cooking dinner, or in the bathroom during that ten minutes you know the kids are glued to the television set watching *Barney*.

Some couples tell me that they "cheat" on the "rules" for

Provocative Encounters during week three and continue making love for longer than ten minutes. There's nothing wrong with that. I also encourage them to consider the time constraint as a vehicle for creating sexual urgency. Not every Encounter has to stop at ten minutes. But knowing that you have just that much time to arouse and satisfy each other makes the sexual relationship feel young, intense, and desperately important again. After two weeks in the program, you will both have changed your sexual attitudes and behavior enough to be open to the prospect of a good erotic encounter in atypical settings *and* in ten minutes.

Remember when you wanted each other so badly but couldn't act on your sexual desire? Provocative Encounters take you back there in a way nothing else can do. Everyone wants to experience that sizzling time again.

## *What to Expect from Week Three*

Desire and arousal will be even higher than in week two. Women who have seldom reached orgasm during intercourse will likely do so in at least one of their Provocative Encounters this week. Men will gain greater confidence in their ability to satisfy their partners. That confidence will allay their fears about sustaining erections or ejaculating too soon.

As couples achieve success in meeting their goals, they also have more fun in planning the Fantasy and Provocative Encounters. They become more playful. It's not unusual for a client to say, "We never laughed during lovemaking before we started this program." And, although the Encounters are planned in advance, they also feel more spontaneous because the partners have learned how to shift positions or activities quickly when something isn't working out. The brevity of the Encounters has an energizing effect on every couple.

Many couples who began the program using low-stimulation Fantasy and Provocative Encounters are ready to turn up the heat considerably in week three. They have overcome their inhibitions and fears about lovemaking. Their physical and emotional responses to each other's kisses and caresses often touch them more deeply than they had anticipated.

Although the third week of the program is generally the most successful for all couples, there are some potential trouble areas.

### *Anxiety*

Couples who start the program with a history of erection difficulties, rapid ejaculation, chronic low desire, inability to become sexually aroused, debilitating performance anxiety, insecurity about their lovemaking skills, or other big issues have the most trouble putting together everything they've learned in the previous weeks to create intensely satisfying sex based primarily on Quickie intercourse positions and incorporating real-life opportunities for sex. Sometimes they focus all their anxiety on the time issue. "We could make this work," they say, "if we had more time for sex."

These couples repeat their initial concern about the program: Provocative Encounters aren't long enough for "good" sex. They say that even while acknowledging they've had good sex in ten minutes the week before. But that was "different," they argue, because this week the emphasis is more solidly on intercourse—in more unusual positions and in everyday situations they hadn't considered "opportunities for sex" before. Now they worry if they really can have good sex in the ten minutes between coming in the door from work and picking up the kids at music lessons.

"We'll never be able to make this work in ten minutes," Nina, thirty-nine, insisted. Her husband nodded in agreement. "It's one thing to have good oral or manual sex in ten minutes, but intercourse? I won't be able to have an orgasm."

Jake, thirty-eight, added, "Last week she came close in one Provocative Encounter. But, this week, with the pressure on, I'm not sure we can do it."

As Jake and Nina talked about their anxiety, they began to laugh. Suddenly they realized that they'd imposed the pressure to perform and to "succeed" on themselves and that they could also take this pressure away. They agreed to plan exciting Fantasy and Provocative Encounters, using new intercourse positions each time. If Nina didn't reach orgasm during the Encounter, Jake would stimulate her manually with his hand or vibrator while talking to her about their Fantasy until she did climax.

With the focus shifted back to creative and arousing lovemaking, Nina and Jake enjoyed the third week of the program and realized their goals. Nina did reach orgasm during one Encounter. The other times, Jake brought her to orgasm manually. "He's much better at doing that now than he was," she said. And, Jake pointed out, Nina was no longer "too embarrassed" to let him satisfy her with his hand or a vibrator.

Often couples who are feeling anxious about their ability to meet their erection and orgasm goals in the last week of the program just need to eliminate their self-imposed deadline pressure. They have to trust that the Fantasy will stir desire and build arousal and that their oral and manual skills can sustain arousal. Even men with a history of losing their erections during intercourse find the erection returns when they stop worrying about it and focus on fantasy and erotic touch.

And if the erection doesn't come back this time or she doesn't reach orgasm, their erotic energy can be redirected into anticipating the next Encounter. Once anxious patients learn to turn negative feelings of anxiety into a positive sexual urgency, they are more likely to have the kind of "success" they want in lovemaking. Always regard an Encounter that didn't end in orgasm as building good sexual tension for next time.

### If You Are Having Problems with Anxiety . . .

Get back in touch with the primary goal: increasing sexual pleasure. *Increasing pleasure*—not reaching orgasm, not sustaining an erection—is the primary goal of the 21-Day Passion Fix program. You're more likely to have successful sexual encounters if you expand the narrow definition of *success* to include "increasing sexual pleasure."

Create a more sexually relaxed atmosphere that is conducive to success. Maybe you're both trying too hard. Inject some laughter into your lovemaking.

Bend the rules and have one Provocative Encounter that is more like one you had last week. Kiss passionately, caress each other while whispering bits of the Fantasy Encounter to one another, and make love by "dry humping" without removing any clothing. It doesn't matter whether he has an erection or whether either of you reach orgasm. The object is to whip up your passions to fever pitch. If you don't experience release, you'll be that much more aroused for the next Encounter. Anticipation builds desire.

Reducing performance pressure for one Encounter will probably make the next one more intense and satisfying.

### *Fear of Sexual Success*

Some couples have as much difficulty dealing with sexual success as others do with failure. They may have an underlying fear of success in general. Men and women who fear success often sabotage themselves in their jobs and relationships—and in their sex lives. Other couples may fear success in the program because they have complicated and conflicting feelings about sexuality. On the one hand, they want better sex or they wouldn't be there. But, on the other hand, they have guilt feelings about enjoying sex.

Whatever the motivating factors, success issues commonly crop up in week three. However, couples rarely identify their problem as a fear of success. They may express concern about being able to continue making progress toward their sexual goals. "We'll never be able to improve on this, so we're doomed to failure" is a common attitude. Or they may revert to making the same excuses about not having the time or the energy for sex that they were making before they started the 21-Day Passion Fix program. For them, success has created performance anxiety.

"We're afraid we won't be able to keep this up," said Angela, thirty-four. Her partner, Ryan, thirty-nine, agreed. "We've met our sexual goals," he said, "but we know we'll backslide. Making progress toward a goal isn't our problem, whether it's working on the house or promising one another to spend more time together. But, we always backslide."

Angela and Ryan had a relationship pattern that many readers will recognize. They let their relationship slide until one or the other got worried about the growing distance between them. He brought home flowers. She made dinner reservations. They planned a romantic getaway. And, for a few weeks or months, they made love often. Then they let other things get in the way. Why? They both felt "guilty" if they spent too much time on each other when they should be pursuing career or family goals, or working on remodeling their Victorian house. They treated sex like a special occasion.

"Whenever things get good, we mess it up," Ryan said. "We'll do it again this time." Angela added, "The last two weeks have been great. The third week can't possibly be as good."

They planned an extra Provocative Encounter at the beginning of the week: a make-out session on the couch in the family room starting twenty minutes before the kids were due home from a sporting event. They pretended they were in week one with no intercourse allowed. As they kissed and caressed, they shared whispered details of their Fantasy. That Encounter put them, they said, "back on track" for the week.

For this couple, the maintenance program (which will be outlined in the next, and final, chapter) was the insurance plan they needed to guarantee they would keep their sexual relationship a top priority.

**If You Are Dealing with Sexual Success Anxiety . . .**

Relax your pursuit of sexual goals. Bend the rules for week three and have a sensual, no-demands Encounter like the one described in the previous section on advice for couples who are anxious about failure. Anxiety may have different causes, but it has similar results.

Talk about your fears to each other. If you and your partner keep talking, you won't be disabled by fear. Ask each other why you are concerned about losing this newly gained sexual ground. If one partner feels guilty about sex, he or she may be able to overcome those feelings more easily for the other's sake.

Don't accept each other's excuses. "This week is too hectic so we'll put off one Provocative Encounter" isn't acceptable. Keep each other motivated.

## Integrating Needs, Desires, and Goals

In some couples, the partners are at different erotic stimulation levels when they enter the program. They may begin the third week still unable to integrate their needs, desires, and goals in a way that feels completely successful to both of them. Often they expect to be evenly matched by now. That's an unrealistic goal. But they can reasonably expect to become *more* evenly matched in the 21-Day Passion Fix program.

Michelle and Ben, in their mid-forties, were anxious about coming to the end of the program without "achieving a perfect sexual fit." She said, "I am still not as adventurous as he would like me to be. I tried a little bondage to please him. It's okay, but not a thrill to me. I felt a little silly being tied to my bed while he teased me with an ostrich feather."

Ben said, "I wish she could get into an experience like that. Her idea of good sex is 'intimate' lovemaking. We have to make eye contact during good old-fashioned intercourse."

Michelle argued correctly that his criticism wasn't justified. She had expanded her repertoire of intercourse positions in week two and was willing to try more Quickie positions, fitting them into their real-life opportunities for sexual contact. They were also learning to compromise in some areas. She was willing, for example, to play at bondage; and he was willing to make love with his eyes open. They agreed to give each other credit for the erotic compromises.

And, they made an important pledge: not to belittle the other's erotic choices. "From now on," Michelle promised him, "I won't tell you I feel silly tied to the bed. I'll put myself into it for the sake of arousing you."

A good sexual relationship isn't a union of clones. If both partners get their sexual needs met often enough, they will be happy.

## If You Are Having Trouble Integrating Needs, Desire, and Goals . . .

Accept that sexual differences exist between you and your partner. Becoming a perfect match is not a requirement for sexual satisfaction. Differences are fine as long as lovemaking consistently is arousing and satisfying to both partners.

Let the phrase, *Cooperate and Compromise*, be your erotic guide. Plan one Provocative Encounter centered around his needs and desires, one around hers.

Complimentary sexual needs can be exciting. Handle

them in a positive way. For example, she can wear sexy lingerie to bed because it turns him on even if it's not her style. What does she get out of dressing up for him? His excitement makes her feel more desirable and builds her arousal as well.

## What If You Haven't Reached Your Sexual Goals by the End of the Week?

Some couples say they are "just getting started" in the third week. They may have had crippling performance problems or inhibitions or long-buried anger and resentment toward each other when they started the program. Occasionally a couple failed to make as much progress as they'd wanted because of a genuine family emergency, such as major illness or death in the family. Even an unplanned but unavoidable business trip can be a setback.

For whatever reason, if you and your partner get to the end of the week three, look at each other, and say, "We really could be where we want to be if we just had another week"— go back and do it again. Here are your options:

- You can repeat the entire program, selecting medium- and high-stimulation Fantasy and Provocative Encounters this time.
- Or you can extend the program by one or two weeks. Again, select higher stimulation Encounters than you did.

James and Darla, a couple in their late thirties, chose to repeat the third week. "We felt we needed one more intense week before we really felt good about achieving our goals," Darla said. "Everyone in our family had head colds during our second week. James and I still kept all our Encounters, but we felt they could have been better."

The fourth week was the charm for this couple. If it's what you need, too, take the extra time. You haven't failed because you need more practice.

## Measuring Your Progress Toward Your Goals

This is your final set of questions in the 21-Day Passion Fix program. Your answers should help you decide if you want to repeat all or part of the program—or move into the maintenance plan, as outlined in the next, and final, chapter.

1. Was the Fantasy Encounter more imaginative and exciting than the previous two—and did it increase tension and desire more quickly?
2. Did incorporating the three Provocative Encounters into real-life time constraints heighten desire and arousal?
3. Were you both more skilled at manually arousing each other?
4. Were you both more skilled at kissing and oral sex—and able to arouse each other more quickly?
5. Did you use sex toys in a more creative way to heighten desire and arousal?

6. Did you try more advanced Quickie intercourse positions—and find them more arousing and satisfying?

7. Were you and your partner orgasmic? Was afterplay more satisfying this week than in the previous weeks?

## Some Quickie Position Suggestions for Week Three

In addition to these positions and the ones already suggested in this book, try positions described in the resources listed on page 151. By week three all couples should be comfortable with medium- and high-stimulation encounters and be comfortable selecting varying levels of intensity as their mood and energy permits.

**The Chair Position.** Use a wide chair, without arms if possible. He sits in the chair. Facing him, she straddles him. He can penetrate her deeply in this position, which is satisfying for both of them. When they're facing each other, they're also in a very intimate position. But they can turn it around if she straddles him, facing away. In this version of the chair position, he can put his arms around her and use his hand to stimulate her clitoris.

**The Pelvic Tilt.** The key to this position is body alignment. Her pelvis needs to be approximately one foot lower than his. Find a place conducive to this alignment, such as the bed, a desk, a countertop, even the hood of a car. She lies back. He stands in front of her. She lifts her legs and rests her feet on his shoulders, tilting her pelvis upward. Her back and pelvis should form a straight line up to his pelvis. He puts his hands under her hips to hold her at this angle while he thrusts. This pelvic tilt provides G spot stimulation during intercourse for her.

**Standing Intercourse.** This urgent intercourse position looks hot in the movies, and it feels just as hot in real life. She is wearing no panties at all or a wispy pair that can be pushed aside as she stands against a wall. He stands in front of her and unzips his pants. As he enters her, she can wrap one leg around his waist. He grasps her buttocks in his hands and thrusts enthusiastically.

# PART SIX

# LIVING
# PASSIONATELY

*Chapter 19*

# The Passion Fix Maintenance Plan

MANY OF MY CLIENTS WORRY that they won't be able to maintain the success they've achieved in the 21-Day Passion Fix program. "We can't sustain this," one woman told me with tears in her eyes. "We will go back to our old ways in a few weeks," her husband said regretfully. Why did they, like many couples, fear losing the ground they'd gained?

They knew they needed the self-imposed discipline and structure of a program to continue enjoying more frequent and exciting sexual encounters. Without that, they were sure they would "fail" again. So many clients expressed this fear to me that I devised a way for them to maintain their success and build on it in the months and years ahead: the Passion Fix Maintenance Program.

The philosophy behind the maintenance program is a simple one: While you can dramatically improve your sex life in only twenty-one days, you probably need a little help from a maintenance plan to hold onto the gains you've made.

Maintenance is a concept familiar to anyone who's ever lost weight. If you're going to keep the weight off, you can't go back to the old eating and (lack of) exercise habits that put you in need of a diet in the first place. On the other hand, you don't need to stay on a strict diet plan. Who can live for the rest of their lives on a diet? Medical experts have been telling us for years that the secret to keeping weight off is a lifestyle change, not the perfect diet. Incorporate healthy eating habits and regular exercise into your life, and you'll never need to diet again. That's "maintenance." The concept has made Weight Watchers an American success story. It can work in your sex life, too.

To keep the Passion Fix working in your sexual relationship, you only need to practice the skills you've acquired and to continue improving and building on them. If you and your partner make the precepts of the 21-Day Passion Fix program a part of your sex life together, you will sustain the passion. And you won't need to schedule one Fantasy Encounter and three Provocative Encounters every week and take a weekly quiz to do that.

I developed a streamlined version of the program, a maintenance plan, at the request of clients to keep them working on their sexual goals long after their twenty-one days are past. And I encourage every reader of this book to use it as well. Most people need some kind of structure to prevent them from falling back into old habits. Without an ongoing commitment to change, the majority of couples will find themselves "too tired," "too busy," and "too stressed" for sex all over again. I set a six-month time period for the maintenance plan, because it generally takes six months for a lifestyle change to become a lifestyle habit, whether the change is exercise or sexual enhancement.

Use the Passion Fix Maintenance Plan for six months following the program—and regular sexual encounters will become a part of your life.

## The Maintenance Plan

Schedule one Fantasy Encounter and one Provocative Encounter per week for six months. At least once a month, fit a Provocative Encounter into a real-life opportunity for sexual contact.

### Fantasy Encounter

Each week's Fantasy Encounter must feature a new and different scenario. Obviously there will be recurring themes in your fantasies, but the story around those themes has to change. And don't feel as though you have to keep topping the last Fantasy with one that is more stimulating, daring, or adventurous. Sometimes you and your partner will want to create a soft, romantic script.

You don't have to keep reaching for higher and higher levels of stimulation to succeed.

### Provocative Encounter

As you did during the three weeks of the program, plan your Encounter to tap into the erotic potential of the Fantasy. Vary the Quickie positions and the ways that you use sex toys. Again, creativity is the key to sustaining passion.

A Provocative Encounter doesn't have to include intercourse every time. If you develop a soft, sensual Fantasy Encounter, for example, you might choose a variation on sensual massage as your Provocative Encounter for the week. There will be weeks when one partner isn't feeling well or has extra job responsibilities or travel. In the past, those situations might have led you to say, "We can't have sex this week."

Now you know that you can have some kind of loving, intimate sex with your partner no matter what else is going on in your life. It may not be the most athletic, daring, and creative sex, but it will be the right kind of lovemaking for your moods and needs at the time. Sex can be soothing and healing as well as passionate and exciting.

## What to Expect from the Maintenance Plan

Most of my clients take my advice and use the maintenance plan after they've completed the program. When they check back with me after six months, they report that the plan helped them solidify gains—and make further progress in achieving their sexual goals. Living the passion has become a reality for them.

"We both feel we might have fallen back into our old habits without the maintenance plan," a male client told me. "We have high-powered jobs, young children, and a lot of other family and community commitments. While we were doing the program, we put a high priority on our sexual relationship. The maintenance plan helped us continue doing that. Without it, we probably would have been too busy for regular sex and glossing over that by promising each other a romantic weekend whenever there was time."

Some clients who weren't completely satisfied with their progress in the program report that the maintenance plan helped them meet their goals. "It put us over the top," a female client explained. "We weren't where we wanted to be after three weeks. Maybe we'd started out with more problems than most couples. But the maintenance plan took us there. After six months, we're really satisfied with our sex life."

Clients have experienced relatively few problems following the maintenance plan. What difficulties they do have fall into two categories: program fatigue and sexual setbacks.

## *Program Fatigue*

Anything can begin to seem like a chore, even sexual enhancement. Some people chafe under the restrictions of any kind of long-term plan. A few clients have said, "Being on a maintenance plan feels like being in school. I agreed to do this for three weeks, not six months. How can you say the program works in twenty-one days and then say, 'Give it another six months'?"

The program *does* work in twenty-one days. The maintenance plan isn't the equivalent of a semester at school or six months in the Army Reserves. It's a gentle reminder to keep up your good sexual habits so you don't lose what you've gained in those twenty-one days.

Steve and Elizabeth, in their mid-thirties, decided after three months that they were "tired of planning Encounters."

"It was beginning to feel like a chore," Elizabeth said, "something else to do on Sunday night at the end of a busy weekend. We skipped two weeks. Then we noticed that we weren't taking advantage of the time we had for Quickies. We weren't putting the same energy into lovemaking that we had been. It wasn't as much fun anymore."

Steve added, "We saw that we were cheating ourselves by not taking the time. It's more my fault than hers that we dropped the plan for a few weeks. I always hate being told what to do. I have dropped out of exercise programs for the same bad reasons. I'm the guy whose gym membership might as well expire halfway through the year. But, we got ourselves back on track."

Getting "back on track" is much easier during the maintenance plan than it was when you started the 21-Day Passion Fix program. You have the skills now. And you know how to use them. Just do it.

### If You Are Suffering from Program Fatigue . . .

Change the way you talk about planning the Encounters. Language affects attitude. Instead of saying, "We have to plan the Fantasy Encounter tonight," try, "I'm looking forward to planning our Fantasy later, and I'm already thinking of ideas. How about you?"

Take a short break. Rather than planning a Fantasy Encounter, talk about fantasies. Reminisce about your past Fantasy Encounters. Read to each other from erotic literature or poetry. Try writing an erotic poem together.

Surprise your partner with a spontaneous Provocative Encounter. If you are more interested in pursuing the plan at the moment than your partner is, take control. Say, "Meet me in the shower in ten minutes. I have a surprise for you."

Plan a Provocative Encounter away from home. Make out for ten minutes in the car in the shopping mall parking lot. Or take a corner booth in a dark bar and play footsies.

### Sexual Setbacks

Occasionally a couple will have a real setback after achieving success in the program and sustaining their achievement for some time in the maintenance plan. These setbacks almost always occur because other factors have put unusual or unexpected stress on the relationship. One client, for example, discovered that her husband had been involved with another woman nearly a year before they started the program. The brief affair was long over, but she was still hurt and angry when she found out about it. She really wasn't "in the mood" for sex with him for quite a while. He understood that and waited patiently until she was ready to try again.

Other couples have reported that traumatic life events, such as the loss of a job or the death of a parent, left one partner reeling and devoid of sexual desire. Many couples have found, however, that their strong sexual connection helps them weather such tough times. A setback, for whatever reason, isn't a failure. It's a challenge you and your partner can face together.

Clark and Terry, in their late forties, overcame sexual performance problems in the program. They were doing well in maintenance. But when Terry was diagnosed with breast cancer three months into the plan, they both felt sex "wasn't as important as her health." "I had the cancerous lump removed, followed by chemotherapy," Terry said. "I didn't look or feel sexy."

"I wanted to hold her and comfort her," Clark said. "I still wanted to make love to her, but she pulled away. Finally she realized that we both needed sex."

Terry and Clark started planning Encounters again, gentle events filled with tenderness and intimate connection. Terry believes those experiences were beneficial to her physical as well as emotional healing process. Now she says, "Sex isn't something any couple can afford to give up when times are hard. Sex changes. Sometimes it's passionate and sometimes it's tender. But we always need some kind of lovemaking in our lives."

### If You Are Experiencing a Sexual Setback . . .

Don't give up sex. Plan low-stimulation Encounters that will help you and your partner sustain a loving, intimate connection no matter what is happening in your lives. Try to plan one Fantasy Encounter and one Provocative Encounter each week, focusing on sensual massage and no-pressure lovemaking.

Let the partner who is feeling stronger plan the Encounters.

When you are both well and emotionally stronger, repeat the 21-Day Passion Fix program.

## *The Six-Month Evaluation*

Give yourself credit for sticking to the plan and having one Fantasy Encounter and one Provocative Encounter a week for six months. If you've done that, you're probably happy with your sex life. Answer the following questions to evaluate your progress in maintaining sexual gains and further realizing sexual goals.

1. Have you been successful in varying the Fantasy Encounters, Quickie intercourse positions, use of sex toys, and Quickie Encounters incorporating real-life opportunities for sexual contact?

2. Have the Fantasy Encounters continued to be imaginative and titillating? Do they continue to increase tension and desire?

3. Does the sensual massage continue to be sexually arousing?

4. Does the manual stimulation continue to be sexually arousing?

5. Is passionate kissing included in most of the Provocative Encounters? Does the kissing continue to be intimate and passionate?

6. Is oral sex included in most Provocative Encounters? Does the oral sex continue to be arousing and satisfying?

7. Are sex toys used in most of the Provocative Encounters? Do they continue to increase desire and arousal?

8. Do the Quickie intercourse positions continue to be arousing and exciting? Each month, have you scheduled at least one Provocative Encounter in a real-life time constraint situation?

9. Does afterplay continue to be satisfying for both partners?

10. Have you successfully maintained attraction, desire, and arousal in your sexual relationship?

11. Are you satisfied with your sexual technique? With your partner's? Has improved technique eliminated or diminished performance anxiety?

12. Have you maintained the improvement you made in sexual communication in the 21-Day Passion Fix program? Are you and your partner more emotionally, and physically, intimate?

Answering these twelve questions will help you determine how well you and your partner have continued to meet and maintain your sexual goals. If you aren't happy with the way you've done that, consider repeating one, two, or three weeks of the program followed by three or six months of the maintenance plan again. Re-evaluate your sexual goals before you begin.

Don't be discouraged if your sex life is not as satisfying as you'd hoped it would be by now. I'm sure you're having more sex, having better sex, and finding more satisfaction in your sexual encounters than you were before you started the program. You're not entirely happy because you want *more*—and there's nothing wrong with that.

I am only concerned about a couple when they say, "We want to give up."

If you've tried unsuccessfully to make the program and the maintenance plan work, consult a sex therapist. You probably need professional guidance and coaching to work through the issues that are getting in the way of great sex for you and your partner. Get help. Don't quit.

## *Why Sex Matters*

When they first come to see me, couples say, "Sex is the first thing to go when we're busy, tired, or stressed." According to a recent survey reported by the NIH, 24 million American women say the same thing. They don't have the time for sex. Or they're too tired for sex. Or, they just aren't "in the mood" for sex.

When you put off sex until later—later can easily become never. Abstinence doesn't make a couple crave sex. It's just the other way around. Sex begets sex.

After couples finish the program, they say, "Once we started having sex on a regular basis, we wanted more sex. We're sexier now. We feel closer to one another, more connected."

Women aren't the only gender who use those words *closer* and *connected*. A male client told me that, two weeks into the program, he wrote his wife a love note and mailed it to her, rather than slipping it into her briefcase. She was touched by his gesture; it was more welcome than a rose.

"I feel so much more connected to you now," he wrote.

That's what sex does for couples. It connects them to each other in an intimate bond that is warm and passionate, tolerant and tender. Couples who have a good sex life forgive each other's imperfections. The 21-Day Passion Fix program has helped you reconnect. The maintenance plan will help you continue to sustain the connection.

I hope you have enjoyed the journey thus far, and I hope you will continue to develop and enjoy your passionate connection for the rest of your lives together.

# Index

defining, 16–19, 210–12
increasing, 68, 218–21
lack of, 131–32
sustaining, 137–41, 217–18

# K

Kegel exercises, 208–9
kissing, 159, 161, 235

# L

lovemaking
*see also* sex
merging differing styles of, 105–6
more creative, 35–36, 45

# M

maintenance plan, 286–93
make-out session, 158–60
manual stimulation, 172–73
massage, 166–67, 230, 234–36
master/slave fantasy, 86–89, 161–62
masturbation, 108, 109, 181–85
men
arousal problems in, 95, 116–17
domineering, 26

# O

oral sex
cunnilingus, 199–201
fellatio, 117, 125–26, 201, 202
increasing, 36, 45–46, 125–26, 181–82
in Provocative Encounters, 198–200, 235–36

orgasms
female, 36, 47–48, 126–30, 191, 204–9, 219–20
problems with, 27–30, 47–48, 191
during Provocative Encounters, 150–51

# P

parenting, stress of, 11–12
Passion Fix program
expectations about, 239, 251, 258–59, 272–73
fatigue with the, 289–92
getting started with, 232–33, 236–38, 239–40
maintenance plan for, 286–93
outline of, 60–67
planning in, 255–56
reasons it works, xv–xvii, 56–58, 67–68, 228–29, 238
six-month evaluation for, 293–95
stimulation levels in, 229–32
week one, 228–50
week three, 269–83
week two, 251–68
performance anxiety, 14–16, 67–68, 116–20, 192–96, 246–48
perineum, 165
phone sex, 112, 189
positions
female superior, 219–22
new, 117, 257, 263–68, 263–68, 282–83
rear entry, 180
Yab-yum, 214–17
power, restoring balance of, 112–14
Provocative Encounters
to achieve orgasm, 204–8

to alleviate boredom, 176–80
blindfold game, 194–96
to build desire, 165–68
components of, 61, 64–66,
149–51, 271–72
to enhance communication, 213–17
erotic competition, 203–4
evaluating, 223–26
female superior position, 219–22
to improve technique, 197–204
to increase arousal, 168–73
to increase attraction, 157–65
introduction to, 146–49
during maintenance plan, 288–89
make-out session, 158–60
massage, 230, 234–36
masturbation, 181–85
oral sex, 198–200
purpose of the, 59–60
to reduce performance anxiety,
192–96
resources for, 151–54
sex toy play, 185–89
suggestions for, 249–50
Tantric sex, 214–17
tie and tease, 162–65
in week two, 257–58

## Q

questionnaire, 7–30
on arousal and performance, 14–16
on communication and intimacy,
16–19
discussing the, 37–38
on frequency and boredom, 23–25
getting partner involved in, 7–8
honesty on, 254
on initiating sex, 25–27

on orgasms, 27–30
on sexual attraction/desire, 10–13
on variety, 20–23
Quickies, xvi–xvii, 59–60, 64–66,
263–68
see also Provocative Encounters

## R

rejection, fear of, 5, 27
relationship
effect of unsatisfying sex life on,
xvii, 138
importance of sex to, 69, 138,
156–57, 191–92, 210–12, 296
problems in, 55–56
resources, 151–54
role-playing, 170–73, 198, 200, 249
role-reversal fantasy, 112–14
romance, xvi, 35, 44

## S

seduction fantasies, 92–94
self-confidence, 109
self-esteem, 19
sex
avoiding, 52–54
communication problems and,
3–5, 55
excuses for not having, 52–56
frequency of, 23–25, 35
importance of, xv, 69, 138,
156–57, 191–92, 191–92,
210–12, 296
initiating, 25–27, 111–14, 185–89
in shower, 249–50
talking about, 6–7, 37–38,
240–42, 259–61

# About the Author

DR. PASAHOW has spent over twenty years practicing as a certified psychoanalyst, certified marriage and family therapist, and certified sex therapist (certification by the American Association of Sex Educators, Counselors and Therapists). Her professional career has been devoted to helping couples achieve sexual intimacy. She is a member and presenter with the American Association of Sex Educators, Counselors and Therapists, the Society for the Scientific Study of Sexuality, the Impotence Institute of America, and holds Diplomat and Supervisory Status with the American Board of Sexology. Dr. Pasahow is also a member of the American Association for Marriage and Family Therapy, the National Association for the Advancement of Psychoanalysis (where she served as a Member of the Board of Trustees), the National Association of Social Workers (Diplomate in Clinical Social Work), and the Academy of Certified Social Workers. She studied under the late eminent Helen Singer Kaplan, M.D., Ph.D., and was part of Dr. Kaplan's clinical team. She is also a frequent lecturer and educator at medical schools, medical practices, and other mental health facilities. Dr. Pasahow has been accepted as a member of the National Registry of Who's Who and has been frequently quoted as an expert on relationships by numerous publications and radio shows. Dr. Pasahow developed the 21-Day Passion Fix program as a response to the needs of her patients. The program's success rate of over 90 percent has been astounding and gratifying to her. She is the only therapist nationwide using this particular form of treatment.

Dr. Pasahow's 21-Day Passion Fix program was a feature article "The Sex Trick Busy Couples Swear By," in the March, 2001 issue of *Redbook* magazine.

Dr. Pasahow manages a successful private practice in Fair Lawn, New Jersey where she and her associates are recognized leaders in both the psychotherapy and sex therapy communities. She currently resides in Wyckoff, New Jersey, with her husband, Jim, and their two young children.